Vegan Interior Design

Aline Dürr

Website: www.veganinteriordesign.com
Email: info@veganinteriordesign.com
LinkedIn: www.linkedin.com/in/veganinteriordesign

Publisher: Aline Dürr
Copy Editor: Steve Cantwell
Cover Design: Vegan Interior Design
Vegan Interior Design Branding & Logo: Daniela Nomura, nomuraportfolio.com
International wholesale enquiries through IngramSparks.
ISBN: 978-0-6489250-0-2 (print), 978-0-6489250-1-9 (e-book)

Table of Contents

vegan [vˈiːɡən] - a way of living which seeks to exclude, as far as possible and practicable, all forms of exploitation of, and cruelty to, animals for food, clothing or any other purpose.

INTRODUCTION

If you are vegan, this book is for you. If you are not vegan, this book is for you too, even more than it is for vegans! That does not mean that I will be waving my finger at you throughout the book and finish off by saying: NOW GO VEGAN! I would much rather for you to consider us two friendly acquaintances having a casual chat over coffee and see me as someone who tells you something new that you did not know yet, simply for the sake of passing on information rather than converting you or convincing you to do something you are not ready to do.

The fact that you picked up this book tells me that you are probably one of three things: concerned about animal suffering, conscious of the impact of factory farms on the environment or aware that a healthy interior environment does not include animal products. If none of these applies, I am still happy that you are onboard and ready to be introduced to a kinder and more sustainable way to treat the world and everyone in it – starting with yourself.

The v-word has a lot of stigma around it and can be controversial. Before I rebranded my company to 'Vegan Interior Design', I weighed up many things and was

1

wondering if I might be automatically shutting people out by including 'vegan' in it. I am sure that this is indeed the case but in the end I decided that it is what it is. Yes, it is plant-based; yes, it is cruelty-free; yes, it is ethical and healthy and sustainable. But all these are just beating around the bush trying not to use the word 'vegan'. They are also not accurate enough as 'cruelty-free' products can still contain animal ingredients. 'Plant-based' means that people may choose a diet based on plants but still buy leather boots and wool rugs. The one and only reason for me to run this business though, is for it to be vegan and to explain vegan interior design to non-vegans. When I was doing research for this book, I found so much interest in the subject but so little information on it. It was professionals around the world that already specialise in vegan interior design in one form or another - be it towel manufacturers making a point of producing their products in a 100% vegan way or kitchen designers who have recognised that vegans have kitchen design requirements that differ from the 'standard' kitchen – that convinced me this is a very much needed subject. The words of Katrina Fox summarise well what I have found whilst writing this book: 'Finally recognized for its positive impact on sustainability and animal welfare without the need to sacrifice taste or style, vegan living is starting to become the norm'. [1]

So why do we even have to link veganism and interior design? Aren't they two completely different things? Isn't veganism just about food? Doesn't veganism only concern a very small number of loud, preaching animal lovers? No – to all of the above. Even the strictest vegan will probably find a few products in this book, he or she never even realised were non-vegan. Animal-derived products sneak into everything and are found where you would least expect them. Veganism and interior design are also very closely linked when it comes to health, as I will explain throughout the book.

In an interview with Magnus Fischer (there is more about the empirical study on veganism and kitchen design in the 'Kitchen' chapter), he mentioned going to a kitchen furniture fair a few years back and being struck by people always talking about 'trends' or 'innovations' when these so-called innovations were really nothing but a repetition of what had already been there before. In the words of Fischer: 'People talk about new surfaces and new materials but the layouts of the kitchens are still the same. Innovation needs to adapt to a new environment and focus on new consumer trends otherwise it's just what is already there. Vegans have a very specific lifestyle and represent a pioneering group with very specific needs.'

Some people say that veganism is just a trend that will pass. This may be true for people adopting a vegan diet for health reasons as they may fall back into old habits. But they were not truly vegan to begin with. If you are vegan for the animals or the environment and you make a point not to include any sort of animal product or by-product into your lifestyle, you know about the cruelty going on behind closed doors. That cruelty does not go away and once you know about it and decide not to be part of it, there is very rarely a way back. It is not another trend that will just come and go like the popularity of velvet upholstery fabric. It is a shift in society and the interior design sector is jumping on board (and needs to catch up quickly).

A lot of this book should be light reading about how to create healthier, happier interiors you surround yourself with: living and work spaces that won't make you sick and that did not make anyone else suffer. Some parts of it, especially the materials part, may be a bit tougher

3

to get through, especially if this is the first time you hear about what animals go through for humans' sake. Please stick around for those parts because you can only make responsible choices when you have the full picture, and it will be worth your while.

I am writing this book without claiming to explain everything exhaustively. There is always more to say, there are always more examples to include. My aim is to give a good overview and summarise the main points of a very complex subject in an easy to digest way. When I mention company, brand or products names, they are just what I came across during my research. I am not affiliated with any of the companies whose products or brands I mention.

I hope this book will be an eye opener for you and provide helpful information that naturally motivates you to change a few (or many) things in your home or business towards healthier, happier and cruelty-free spaces.

'Lead with the carrot not with the stick. It's not about chastising people or telling them that they are doing something wrong, it's all in the education of people. The whole process of veganising interior design is a constant learning for us designers as well. We do not specifically advertise ourselves as vegan designers. If we give information or if we offer vegan materials, it is usually a 100% uptake from the clients because they buy into the new information we give them and are really interested in it.'

Jordan Cluroe and Russell Whitehead from 2LG Studio London

4

'I always wondered why somebody
doesn't do something about that. Then I
realised I was somebody.'
-Lily Tomlin

Why Vegan Interior Design

Rising Awareness

Veganism is gaining popularity and is widely practised by more and more people every day. While the numbers may still seem small, veganism has grown to 2.5% of the US population in 2019, up from only 1% in 2009.[2] The number of vegans in Great Britain quadrupled between 2014 and 2019, from 150,000 to 600,000.[3] 5% of Israelis are now following a vegan lifestyle, as are 3% of Italians, 4% of Swedes and 3% of Swiss.[4] Google searches for 'veganism' have increased by 580% over the last five years.[4] 'Veganism' as a term has received almost five times more interest at the end of 2019 than 'vegetarian' and 'cruelty-free' searches combined.[4] There are many more numbers to prove my point but I will leave it at that for now.

You may be surprised to know though, that veganism is not really a new thing. It has existed under many different names throughout history. Although it may be much older than written history, veganism was officially introduced to the world in the writings of ancient Greece and India. Greek philosophers were said to practise abstinence from all meats and animal products. Early Hindus also practised veganism as part of ancient Hindu traditions.

Since ancient times, veganism has existed in some form, even if it was only practised by a small number of religious ascetics or adherents. In the United States and England, veganism had already gained popularity by the early 1800s. Throughout the nineteenth century, veganism was often prescribed by physicians as a cure for many different illnesses. Due to its tremendous health benefits, there have been societies, communities and schools established in the name of furthering the vegan cause. The name itself is a twentieth century invention, but call it what you will, veganism has existed for millennia.

'With non-vegans being interested in cruelty-free interior design it is a bit like with animal tested toiletries and cleaning products. Many people don't use them but still eat meat. Avoiding animal products in interiors is not a vegan only issue. Many people realise there is cruelty involved and want to avoid it.'

Chloe Bullock, materialise interiors Brighton

For several years now, vegan living has been going mainstream and is starting to become more normal because it is more and more recognised for its positive impact on the environment and animal welfare. People realise that they do not need to practise an extreme and restricted lifestyle; and they do not need to sacrifice taste, style or comfort for their beliefs and values. While the vegan food sector is still growing tremendously all over

7

the world, vegan fashion has been catching up over the last few years. A natural motivation to use cruelty-free and sustainable materials and products is spreading widely. The People for the Ethical Treatment of Animals (PETA) Vegan Homeware Awards have been celebrating vegan products, brands and designers at the top of their game for four years in a row, with winners including the likes of Ikea, H&M, Zara Home and Luxury Italian furniture brand Cassina in collaboration with Philippe Starck.

According to Deborah diMare, interior decorator, author, speaker and influencer for the compassionate & healthy design movement, there are about 180 million socially conscious consumers in the US today; 56 per cent of Americans will not consume products that they believe are unethical.[5] She points out that socially conscious consumers are slowly outgrowing the traditional ones and that connecting with them and incorporating their values into one's business will help to reach the conscious market.

'It's a brave new business world, one in which growing numbers of consumers will continue to demand sustainable and ethical products. If you're about to start a business, it's worth making your products vegan-friendly from the start. If you already have a business, consider veganizing it by removing any animal-based ingredients or components. Going a step further by gaining certified vegan status from the Vegan Society (UK) or Vegan Action (US) will help to set your brand apart from those that merely pay lip service to ethics.'[1]

Katrina Fox, Founder of Vegan Business Media and the Plant Powered Women's Network

Photo by Hutomo Abrianto

For the interior design industry, a significant and steadily growing target group with specific functional, emotional and social needs has developed. Textile and furniture manufacturers who may not yet have thought about the ethical aspects of their materials will have to do so. While the use of leather or animal derived glues may be simply a matter of habit and availability, consumers are asking more and more questions. With quality vegan materials appearing on the market left, right and centre, there is a need for cultural change among developers and manufacturers. Whether it is luxury fashion, automotive design or upholstery, vegan alternatives to leather, wool and silk are appearing everywhere. We are seeing the creation of leather alternatives made from pineapple waste, apple peels, mushrooms, flowers, cacti and even wine. We see vegan silk made from citrus peels and banana tree stalks. We see liquid coconut waste from the food industry turned into cellulose offering an environmentally friendly alternative to wool. While some of these products may still seem a bit futuristic, the market is accelerating.

'Responsible consumerism is of great importance among the conscious lifestyle groups. They are less price-sensitive and willing to spend more money on products considered important for them than the general population.'[6] The vegan target group is, if convinced, very loyal and spreading the word. The vegan community is not keeping silent, they have the urge to speak out and share their views.[7]

So why exactly is the vegan market growing so fast? In the next three chapters I will give you an insight into the main three drivers: ethics, sustainability and health.

'In any moment of decision, the best thing you can do is the right thing, the next best thing is the wrong thing and the worst thing you can do is nothing'.
-Theodore Roosevelt

Ethics

The suffering of billions of animals each year in factory farming, referred to as one of the 'worst crimes in history' by Yuval Noah Harari in a Guardian article in 2015 [8], is the most powerful motivation for many people to become vegan. Ethical vegans refuse to support a system that abuses, tortures and kills billions of innocent lives each year. They consider the avoidable use of animals and animal by-products to be inconsistent with living free from causing harm. By choosing a vegan lifestyle, people recognise that animals are not theirs to use in any way. Having emotional attachments with animals may form a part of that but it is mainly the understanding that all sentient creatures have a right to life and freedom that motivates ethical vegans to live how they live. There is always talk about 'humane slaughter' or using animal by-products from the meat industry for more sustainability. At the end of the day, though, you cannot kill someone humanely who did not want to die; and ultimately, any product or by-product that comes from an animal, who by the way has not given anyone permission to use its body for their own use, stems from one form of cruelty or another. In a vegan space, you will not find anything reminding you of blood, torture or death.

Another angle that may not necessarily be considered by people that are vegan for the animals, but that is equally important to raise, is the ethical consideration to the humans working in businesses such as slaughterhouses, shearing sheds and tanneries (not to mention the entire communities living in the neighborhoods of the tanneries). Mental and physical health issues, domestic violence and early deaths are a common theme in these industries, as I will discuss further in the 'Materials' section.

'You cannot do a kindness too soon,
because you never know how soon it will
be too late.'
-Ralph Waldo Emerson

Health

M any people adopt a vegan diet for health reasons. While there is a lot of proof that a vegan diet reduces the risk of heart disease, high blood pressure, diabetes and cancer, I want to focus on the health implications of vegan and non-vegan materials with which people surround themselves.

Our health is not only determined by our diet and fitness; it is also hugely affected by our direct environment. We can design spaces that reduce stress, anxiety and an overall negative state of health. When it comes to workplace design, this is something that has been in the spotlight in recent times. To a certain extent, most people are aware that the layout, lighting, acoustics, furnishings and air quality do affect the overall feel of a space, be it an office or a home. Recently, there is also more awareness about materials and fabrics and their effect on our health.

If you look at fur, wool, leather or down, none of them is healthy in a home or office environment - the opposite is true in fact. All the above materials are only natural on the animal born with them. Once you remove an animals' coat, skin or feathers, they need to be treated with a toxic concoction of chemicals to make sure that they will not start rotting in the buyer's home, be it in their wardrobe, in their pillows or in their lounge. Allergies, feather duvet lung, asthma, hormonal imbalances and different forms of cancer are only a few possible adverse health effects of animal-derived materials and products in a home and people are looking for alternatives. Vegan interior design

15

focuses on environments that promote good health and well-being while respecting animals and the planet.

Just because a material is vegan, it does not necessarily mean that it is healthy though. Low-quality man-made materials can contain plenty of toxic chemicals as well. This will be discussed in detail when you get to the 'Materials' section.

Photo by Minh Pham

'Let's face it, being ahead of one's time is always inconvenient; but if nobody forged ahead despite inconvenience, nothing would ever change for the better.'
-Victoria Moran

Sustainability

Vegans 'for the environment' know that one of the most effective ways for every individual to lower their carbon footprint is to avoid all animal products and by-products. They know that using reusable coffee cups, recycling, composting, cycling to work and using as little plastic as possible will reduce the impact on their environment; but they also know that greenhouse gas emissions produced by livestock are doing more harm to the climate than all modes of transportation combined. [9] And the problem goes beyond cow and sheep flatulence.

Photo by Toa Heftiba   Photo by Sylvie Tittel   Photo by Pop & Zebra

One single sheep can produce up to 30 litres of methane every single day. This means that gases passed by animals, mostly sheep, in New Zealand alone make up more than 90 per cent of the nation's total methane emissions[10]. Intensive fur farms create ridiculous amounts of manure which result in greenhouse emissions, nutrient flows and loss of biodiversity. The waste runoff from intensive fur factory farms is contaminating soil and waterways and creates a major pollution problem. Toxic chemicals used in leather tanneries are flushed into local rivers and lakes affecting whole communities by polluting the water people drink and poisoning the fish they eat. The production of any type of animal product places a heavy burden on the environment. The enormous amount of grain needed for meat and leather production is a major culprit of deforestation, habitat loss and species extinction. It is not only the Amazon that has been bulldozed for over 30 years; land is being cleared all over the world to make room for grazing animals. This leads to increased soil salinity and erosion, with approximately 20 per cent of pastureland worldwide considered degraded due to overgrazing.

'In the first half of the 20th century, Argentina was second only to Australia in wool production. But when local Argentinean sheep farmers got too greedy, the scale of their operations outgrew the capacity of the land to sustain them. Soil erosion in the region has triggered a desertification process that officials estimate threatens as much as 93 per cent of the land. Today, Argentina is no longer a major wool producer – and Australia could suffer a similar fate.' [10]

PETA Australia

'Do the best you can until you know better. Then when you know better, do better.'
-Maya Angelou

No Black & White

Like with everything in life, you need to weigh up which bad is worse than another, but doing something good – choosing one vegan product over an animal-derived product at a time – is better than just keeping doing what you have always done. There will always be trade-offs and, like everywhere else in life, there are plenty of grey areas in vegan life and design. Here is one example:

If you buy a cheap synthetic blanket from a large retailer then it is great that it is not wool and no animal was harmed in the production. But what about the sweat shop worker who made it? What about the life cycle of the synthetic fibres which are made from petroleum and will ultimately end up in landfill and pollute the environment?

It is true that many faux-leathers or faux-furs are plastic based and it is a fact that plastic is very bad for the environment. However, they do not require the land needed to raise and feed the animals, nor do they require tanning and bleaching of the hides and pelts; so overall their production is less toxic, creates less pollution and prevents the destruction of land – objectively, they are the lesser evil.

'It would be great if there were more high-end eco-friendly material alternatives because when it comes to fabrics in general there is just so much waste. I think a lot of materials are manufactured in third world countries which do not have the same manufacturing standards and limitations. So, you know you are doing a good thing if you buy an alternative to animal-derived materials by not hurting animals but you ask yourself what does this alternative material really do to the environment?'

Tatum Kendrick, Studio HUS Los Angeles

An important point to consider is that every individual is at a different stage in life. Some may just be interested in veganism, others are already trying to be vegan and others may be very strictly vegan. We all have very different priorities and, as discussed above, the motivations for being vegan can differ widely: some are vegan for the animals, some for the environment and others strictly for health reasons. As a result, vegan interior design is not an all or nothing approach. You can do the best you can using the knowledge that you have at the stage you are at. If you take one step at a time, keep learning and educating yourself and applying what you have learned the way you feel is best, it still has a huge impact.

'When I onboard new clients I have a form they fill in where I get to grip with the types of specifications they might be interested in. All are willing to go with lower impact to animals and planet - providing it doesn't add cost. It's surprising that responses are not predictable. For instance, a client might not want animal tested paint but happy to have petrochemical paint rather than natural paint. We are all different – even vegans.'

Chloe Bullock, materialise interiors Brighton

'To close your eyes will not ease
another's pain.'
-Ancient Chinese Proverb

Materials & Finishes

As I have said before, this book is not meant to scare or upset you. The truth behind animal-derived products, no matter if they are food based or material based, is cruel. It is cruel because the worldwide demand for leather and wool, milk and eggs, down and fur, meat and silk cannot be met by romantic, beautiful small-scale animal farming as it is portrayed in my 2-year-old daughter's picture books. Approximately 1 billion animals are killed every year for leather and hides alone.[11]

I have tried to describe the 'production' of leather, wool, down, fur and silk in a digestible way, but facts are facts and if you have a heart for animals, or compassion for all kinds of beings, the next chapters may surprise and even shock you. Please stay with me as the alternative materials shown at the end of each chapter will be easy to swap in to replace the cruel ones – mostly at no additional cost and with the same level of comfort and luxury.

One more point I would like to make is that just like there are many different levels of veganism, there are obviously also different levels of vegan interior design. There is an entry level in which people simply swap as many cruel materials as possible with cruelty-free materials. This level makes a MASSIVE difference for the animals and the environment and is a big leap forwards from the traditional ways.

At a more advanced level, people do not only swap cruel materials with cruelty-free ones but also look at the bigger scope. It includes sustainability concerns and looking into how cruelty-free products may indirectly impact the environment and the animals in a negative way – making them less cruelty-free than they may appear at first glance. It means ditching all sorts of materials made with petrochemicals, forms of plastic and other substances that are harmful for our planet and everyone in it. Due to a lot of misleading information and marketing strategies, as well as very complex and secretive manufacturing processes, it can be really hard to determine if a product is as cruelty-free, healthy and sustainable as it seems to be.

In terms of change, some people may just start with five to ten animal-based items that are simple to replace, others do a radical clear out. Some cannot stand the thought of having anything dead or animal-derived in their homes once they find out about the cruelty behind it, some do not want to throw out and waste something perfectly functional until it breaks. In my eyes, it does not really matter what level you are at. Everyone has got their own timeline and way of doing things; the most important thing is that you make informed choices. The following chapters are meant to give you a starting point and enough information to realise that a shift from our traditional ways is necessary for multiple reasons.

'The question is not 'can they reason' nor
'can they talk?' but 'can they suffer?''
-Jeremy Bentham

LEATHER

Myth 1: Leather is a by-product

Myth 2: Leather is organic and sustainable

Myth 3: Leather usually comes from cows

Facts

Leather is probably the most obvious non-vegan and 'cruel' material that is used in interior design. What is so bad about it? Yes, it is the skin of a dead animal, but isn't it just a by-product and the animals died for food anyway? Unfortunately not! It is a common misconception that leather comes from cows that are being killed for meat. You have probably been told that you are doing a good thing when you buy leather because at least the skin of a dead cow did not go to waste, which makes it sustainable. The truth, however, could not be further from that.

To start with, leather is not a by-product. What will shock you even more is that the leather used for clothing, shoes, car interiors and furniture does not only come from dead cows but also very commonly from dogs, cats, seals, goats, deer, ostriches, lambs, buffalos and kangaroos. They are all bred, tortured and killed for the sole purpose of using their skin for decorative purposes. There is virtually no way to tell what kind of animal the leather you are wearing or sitting on came from. Even if a product says that it was made in Italy the raw materials came, most likely, from India or China.

Leather production is an industry in itself – a very large and profitable one. So I'll repeat it one more time: leather is not a by-product! The leather industry in Bangladesh alone is worth billions of dollars a year.

Photo by Hannah Busing

Now that you know that, let's get into some more gruesome details which are necessary for you to know to get the whole picture. If we take cow leather production in Brazil, for example (Brazil is the second largest leather producing country in the world), the typical order of things would be similar to this: a female cow is forcefully impregnated by a farmer sticking their arm up inside her. She then carries and grows her calf for nine long months of pregnancy, just as long as a human mother carries her baby. Once the calf is born it is usually taken away right away or within the next 48 hours (there may be farms that handle it differently but I am speaking about common international practice here). After the calf has been taken from its mother it will be kept in a tiny crate isolated from others, usually exposed to the elements and barely able to move, for about two to three years. Female cows are then used to continue the cycle and artificially impregnated to produce more babies. Males are loaded onto trucks and shipped to slaughterhouses that are up to 48 hours away. The trucks are overcrowded and there is no water or food. On arrival at the slaughterhouse, they are sent to the 'knock box' where they are knocked unconscious with different torturous tools. Unfortunately, in many cases they are still fully conscious when they are loaded onto the slaughter line, where their body parts are hacked off one by one and the animals are skinned.[5]

The leather production in India is very well summarised in the documentaries *Earthlings* (2005) and *Dominion* (2018) and well described in an article by Peter Popham for *The Independent*.[12] In India, cows are 'sacred' and their special status is enshrined in law in most states except Kerala, Goa, West Bengal and states of the Northeast India. This leads to a huge amount of cattle trafficking, mainly to West Bengal and Kerala, as well as neighbouring Bangladesh. For some of the way, the cows are transported by truck or train, but for a large part they have to walk to their own death at a slaughterhouse. While the law allows for four cows to be transported per truck, up to 70 are usually put in.[12] Train wagons are allowed to hold 80–100 cows; however, up to 900 are usually crammed in with up to half of them arriving dead. Once the cows are unloaded, a long and painful march begins for them. 10,000–15,000 cows EACH DAY are crossing the border to Bangladesh alone. To keep them moving, they are beaten with sticks and they are not allowed to rest or drink.[13] When they sink to their knees in exhaustion, they are violently pulled by their nose ropes and their tails are twisted or broken to force them back up. If that does not work the drivers rub hot chili peppers or tobacco into their eyes to keep them awake and moving.[13] The cruelty does not end there. Due to the enormous amount of walking, the cows lose a lot of weight, so in order to increase the weight at their final destination, and the amount of money received per cow, the traffickers give them water laced with copper sulphate. This destroys their kidneys and makes it impossible for them to pass water. Finally, at the slaughterhouse, they are tied up and their heads are beaten to a pulp with the help of a hammer. It is hard to swallow, but this is where most leather comes from. This may be enough information to make you stop and think about your actual need for leather but for those who may require some more graphic material to make the connection, the documentary *Earthlings* is depicting standard practices in leather production quite well.

The largest leather-producing country is China. Almost all dog and cat leathers come from China, even though the import of dog and cat skins is banned and illegal in most countries. Unfortunately, distinguishing their leather from cow, sheep and pig leather is almost impossible. As you can imagine, the production of dog and cat leather is no less cruel than for any other animal. After being locked up in tiny cages without food or water, cats and dogs are usually grabbed around the neck with metal pinchers before being bashed over the head with a wooden pole. While some fall unconscious, others cry out in agony with severe head trauma. Even after their throats are cut, some still struggle to breathe and are conscious while their skins are ripped off.

Source: VEGANDESIGN.ORG

All of the above is horrifying and hard to read! It is also just a small snippet of the leather industry, but I believe it is enough to demonstrate that there is no 'ethical' leather. No sentient being, no matter how 'well kept' and cared for, wants to die so that you can sit on its skin. Leather is cruel no matter how you label it.

If the truth about the pain and torture that animals have to go through for the production of leather has not shocked you enough, let us look into the human toll of the leather industry. I will start with a fact: a report by the Bangladesh Society for Environmental and Human Development says 8,000–12,000 tannery workers aged 30-35 years suffer from gastrointestinal disease, dermatological disease, hypertension (12%) and jaundice (19%).[14] Ninety per cent of tannery workers die before the age of 50. The majority of tanneries where raw skins are turned into leather are located in India and Bangladesh, where labour is cheap and where there is very little legislation on the dangerous handling of toxic substances. Chrome tanning is the most popular form of producing leather these days. It relies on a poisonous concoction of chromium salts and tanning liquor. Workers are exposed to these toxic substances all day with no protection whatsoever.

What is worse is that these toxic chemicals used in the tanneries are flushed into local rivers and lakes, affecting whole communities by polluting the water people drink and poisoning the fish they eat. Not only does wastewater from tanneries contain flesh, hair, mould and faeces, but the chromium, lead and arsenic-laced water causes issues such as respiratory problems, asthma, skin rashes, infections, infertility, tuberculosis and birth defects. Half a million residents of Hazaribagh Bangladesh alone are at risk of serious illness due to chemical pollution from tanneries near their homes.[14] Even in fully modernised and carefully managed facilities, it is nearly impossible to reclaim all of the pollutants generated by the tanning process. And, of course, it is not only waterways that are polluted by the tanning process; carcinogens, methane, toxic greenhouse gases like ammonia and other poisons are emitted into the air as well.

There has been ongoing research trying to find alternative tanning methods that are more human- and environmentally friendly such as using plant extracts and enzymes. In fact, vegetable tanning is the most traditional method of tanning leather that uses natural tannins such as woods, barks, fruits, pods and leaves. While this may remove some of the dangerous toxins from the leather production, you still sit on the skins of dead animals that had to be preserved from rotting away under you in one way or another and the chemical method is still the most widely used.

So yes, you could argue the tanneries create jobs, but what good does a job if it hurts the worker and his entire community?

Photo by Federico Gutierrez

Adverse Health Effects

While some people prefer not to think about where the materials they love have come from and who has been hurt in the process of making them, everyone has an interest in their own health. If you buy a leather couch, you are not only sitting on dead animals but also on the remnants of cyanide, formaldehyde, chromium and many other toxic chemicals day in, day out. They soak into your skin and make their way into the respiratory system.[15] Leather furniture can off-gas for years, which means you continue to breathe in chemicals as you work, sleep and relax in your home or office. Just like tannery workers, only in a slightly less concentrated form, you are exposed to long-term off-gassing from many harmful chemicals that are used in leather production.

Leather Alternatives

Let us look at some positives after all these gruesome facts and details. With so many leather alternatives coming to the party over the last years, the global leather industry is expected to experience a radical upheaval. I do not claim that these alternatives are widely and easily available in every country of the world and there are also many other options. These are just some of the alternatives you should be looking out for:

Pineapple Leather

The raw material that forms the base of pineapple leather is a by-product of the pineapple harvest. The pineapple leaf fibre is mixed with a corn-based polylactic acid and undergoes a mechanical process to create a non-woven mesh. The felt is coloured using Global Organic Textile Standard (GOTS) certified pigments and a resin top coating is applied to give additional strength, durability and water resistance.

Mango Leather

Mango leather is solving two problems (animal cruelty and fruit wastage) in one product, transforming leftover fruit into durable, leather-like material. It is a very eco-friendly material which can be dyed to the preferred colour. In the production of the raw material natural additives are used to make the fruit-leather sheets.

Apple Leather

Similar to mango leather, apple leather is made of food waste and consists of 50 - 70 per cent apple pulp, using everything that is left over after pressing apples for juice or cider. The other 30-50 per cent is made up of sustainably sourced ingredients. The production process is free from toxic chemicals and all ingredients are plant-based and eco-friendly.

Flower Leather

'Fleather' is made from upcycled flowers and provides a sustainable alternative to plastic-based materials. A consortium of natural organisms is allowed to grow over a flower-based nutritive substrate over a period of three weeks, when the 'fleather' is formed. It is 100 per cent biodegradable and upcycles a product that would otherwise be wasted.

Cactus Leather

Made of nopal cactus leaves, this leather is organic and all-natural without any toxic chemicals, phthalates or PVC. It has a great softness of touch while offering solid performance for a wide variety of applications. It is partially biodegradable and has the technical specifications required by the furniture and even automotive industries.

Wine Waste Leather

The main ingredients of wine leather are waste products of Italian wine production. Grape marc consists of grape skins, stalks and seeds discarded during wine production. No toxic solvents, heavy metals or substances which are dangerous for humans or the environment are involved in the production process. Wine leather is soft, smooth, stable, sustainable and recyclable. The material is produced in different thicknesses, elasticities, weights, finishings, textures and backing textiles.

Mushroom Leather

Mushroom leather comes from a big parasitic fungus that grows in the wild and attacks the trees in subtropical forests. It has a soft touch similar to suede and its consistency and texture goes from soft to slightly harder than cork. The total absence of toxic substances makes it ideal for use in close-to-skin applications and it also limits bacteria proliferation. Mushroom leather has the capacity to absorb moisture and then to release it in a short time, just like a fabric. It is not waterproof in its natural form but it can be treated with eco wax.

'There is no fundamental difference
between man and animals in their ability
to feel pleasure and pain, happiness, and
misery.'
-Charles Darwin

WOOL

Myth 1 - Sheep need to be shorn anyway

Myth 2 – Shearing does not hurt the sheep

Myth 3 – Wool is an organic product

Facts

It is true that sheep need to be shorn. However, nature did not intend it this way; it is human manipulation which makes this a necessary procedure. Without human interference, sheep would produce just enough wool to protect themselves from extremes of temperature. The amount of wool sheep grow these days has been genetically manipulated. Merino sheep, for example, are bred to have extra folds of skin so that they produce more wool. In Australia, where about one quarter of the world's wool is produced, this unnatural excess wool causes many Merino sheep, who are native to Spain and not made for Australian temperatures, to collapse and die from heat exhaustion during the summer months. The extra skin also leads to moisture retention which invites flies to lay eggs in the wrinkles, referred to as flystrike. Flystrike can produce inflammation and general systemic toxaemia, and causes the death of around three million sheep a year in Australia alone. In an attempt to reduce the risk of flystrike, a painful procedure called mulesing is still widely used despite international criticism and continuous attempts to phase out the cruel practice. Usually carried out when a lamb is between six and ten weeks of age, mulesing involves cutting flaps of skin from around a lamb's bottom and tail using sharp shears. New Zealand banned mulesing in 2018. However, many Australian farmers continue to mutilate lambs as it is faster and cheaper than the more humane alternatives. This primitive method to prevent maggot infestations is not only cruel, it is also unnecessary as sheep can be protected through methods such as shearing wool under the tail, controlling flies in the environment, closer monitoring and spray washing.

Other practices of 'marking' a lamb include tail docking, castration, ear notching or ear tagging. These are performed without anaesthesia or pain relief. While all of these operations are quick for the executor, the acute pain for the lambs can last several weeks.

Photo by Simon Infanger

Another sad result, which is, however, more related to breeding sheep for meat rather than wool alone, is the fact that approximately 15 million lambs – one out of four – die within 48 hours of birth every year in Australia alone. This is the result of many sheep being manually impregnated at an unnatural time of the year. They then give birth during the winter months, which allows their babies to be weaned in time for spring when the fields are most fertile so that they can fatten up before being slaughtered for the Christmas season. Industry standards do not require any form of shelter and tiny lambs born on frozen paddocks, with no protection from the elements, have limited chances of survival. What adds to the problem is that sheep farmers have access to genetics technology that ensures sheep will carry twins or triplets – and sometimes even up to six lambs at a time. As well as these lambs often being simply too weak and small to survive, many mothers do not survive the birth themselves.

Photo by Sam Carter

A word about shearing: while it should just feel like a haircut, countless instances of undercover footage and ex-shearers' reports prove that sheep get badly cut, kicked, have their legs broken, or suffer their teats, tails or ears being cut or torn off during the shearing process. With shearers being paid by volume, they are encouraged to work as quickly as possible with little to no regard for the sheep's welfare. Australian media have documented that many workers take illegal drugs to help them work even faster.[16] The sheep's physical and mental health suffers and they are rarely treated with pain killers after the abusive procedure.

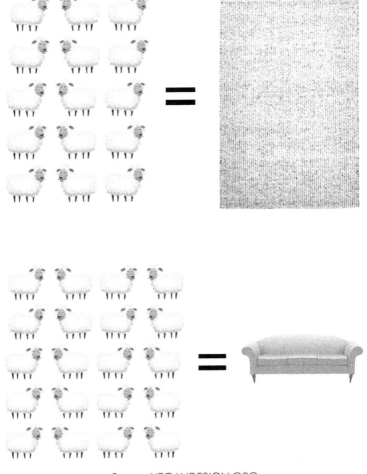

Source: VEGANDESIGN.ORG

41

Sheep are not alone in this. Recent PETA undercover footage shows that alpacas are hit, kicked, tied down and mutilated in Peru by the world's top alpaca producer.

'The workers pulled alpacas up off the floor by the tail and yanked them around. According to one veterinary expert who reviewed the footage, such "excessive force applied to the bones, joints, and soft tissues in the area" would cause dislocations, fractures, and severe permanent nerve damage. They also slammed pregnant alpacas onto tables. Workers tied them tightly by the legs into a restraining device reminiscent of a medieval torture rack and pulled hard, nearly wrenching their legs out of their sockets. Restraint is highly distressing to alpacas, who are prey animals and fear that they are about to be killed. Terrified of being pinned down and totally defenceless, they cried out, spit, and vomited in fear as workers grabbed them by the ears. Afterward, the workers threw them onto the concrete floor and even stood on their necks. Some alpacas froze for several minutes, apparently exhausted after their ordeal.'[17]

PETA UK

Cashmere goats are another animal exploited and tortured for their hair. Nearly all cashmere comes from Mongolia or China where workers have been witnessed holding down and stepping on frightened goats, bending their legs into unnatural positions as they were tearing out their hair using sharp metal combs.[18] Just like sheep, goats are left with gaping wounds and bloody cuts without pain relief or veterinary care. There are no regulations or penalties for animal abuse on cashmere farms and, after being tortured over and over again, animals that are no longer deemed profitable are either left to bleed out with their throats slit or violently killed by hammers smashed into their heads.

As mentioned in the Sustainability chapter, wool production is not as organic as it is made out to be. In fact, it is absolutely devastating for the environment. Methane and greenhouse gases; pollution of land and water by manure, pesticides, chemicals and run-off waste; decreased biodiversity; deforestation; degrading of pastureland; and soil erosion – these are only some of the results of excessive sheep farming.

Cashmere has an even more destructive impact on the environment and climate with cashmere goats eating roots of grasses, preventing regrowth and contributing to soil degradation and desertification. 'Already, 65 percent of Mongolia's grasslands are degraded, and 90 percent of Mongolia is in danger of desertification, which has led to some of the world's worst dust storms on record and air pollution dense enough to reach North America.'[18]

Adverse Health Effects

There is not much conclusive scientific research on wools' effect on our skin but there is enough scientific evidence that wools are the perfect breeding grounds for dust mites that can cause asthma and other respiratory issues in our homes. Being sensitive to wool materials is very common, especially in young children, and people report runny noses, watery eyes, skin irritations and rashes when they wear or touch wool. Recent data has identified a specific component of lanolin being the actual cause of many people's discomfort when wearing wool.[19] It was also found that wool allergies have increased over the past decade making it more common than first suspected.

43

Wool Alternatives

Organic Cotton

(only GOTS certified, see 'Textile' chapter for more information)

Organic cotton is grown without harmful chemicals and does not destroy ecosystems. It is known to improve soil quality and often uses less water than traditional cotton production. Like other vegan fabrics, organic cotton is easier to clean than wool, faster drying and softer to the touch.

Soybean Fibre

Soybean fibre is made from the hulls of soy beans and is often known as 'vegan cashmere'. This eco-friendly fabric is free of petrochemicals and offers the comfort of cashmere, the softness of silk and the durability of cotton.

Tencel

Tencel is a cellulose fibre which is made by dissolving wood pulp and using a special drying process called spinning. Before it is dried, wood chips are mixed with a solvent to produce a wet mixture. The mixture is then pushed through small holes to form threads, which are then chemically treated. The lengths of fibre are spun into yarn and woven into cloth. TENCEL™ lyocell and modal fibers are certified as compostable and biodegradable, thus they can fully revert to nature. They are also certified by the international Oeko-Tex Standard 100 as they are not containing harmful substances.

Bamboo

If grown in the right conditions, bamboo can be very sustainable - but try to steer clear of rayon, a highly chemical-intensive bamboo-derived material.

Woocoa

An innovative material created by a group of university students in Colombia, Woocoa is a coconut and hemp fibre 'wool' treated with enzymes from the oyster mushroom. It is not widely commercial yet, but it is an exciting development for the future.

Nullabor

Bacteria are used to naturally ferment liquid coconut waste from the food industry into cellulose, which is the building block for the final product. It is created in just 18 days and requires very little water, land or energy.

Hemp

This natural, biodegradable material is often used in blended fabrics and does not require any pesticides to grow, which makes it ideal for organic farming. It is also very breathable and does not trap heat like wool does, thus avoiding the growth of bacteria.

Banana Silk

Banana silk yarn is made from the very long fibres of the banana leaf, producing a high sheen, soft and yet very strong silky fibre. Banana leaves must be harvested as part of the regular banana fruit production, making banana silk yarn a resourceful application of this by-product.

'The soul is the same in all living creatures, although the body of each is different.'
-Hippocrates

DOWN AND FEATHERS

Myth 1: Animals are not harmed by gathering feathers

Myth 2: Birds are naturally moulting

There is nothing better than snuggling into a warm blanket at the end of the day and sinking your head into a comfortable cushion. For me personally, the lighter and fluffier the blanket the better. This is why down was a straightforward choice for me until I found out what I was actually covering myself with. Reading about it was one thing but watching the footage on geese in the documentary *Dominion* and hearing and seeing their pain was what really did it for me. I happened to foster two ducks from the pound at that time, and witnessing their beautiful, gentle personalities while gaining knowledge about the cruelty executed towards their kind in other countries broke my heart.

Facts

The majority of the world's down supply comes from live-plucked ducks and geese in China. What does live plucking mean? It means that fully conscious birds are pinned upside down every six to eight weeks while their thickest and deepest plumage and undercoating is ripped out of their skin. If you think this would probably only hurt as much as ripping out a hair, think again. Ripping out an entire plumage is extremely painful and traumatising for the animals. It results in serious tissue injuries, torn ligaments and broken limbs and wings. In order to restrain the birds, their legs may be tied up, with 'live-rippers' stepping on their wings or putting them in choke holds. Not being able to breathe with the pressure being applied to their chests, they experience the fear of suffocation and being smothered. Sick or injured birds are considered wastage and are left to die untreated. While the natural lifespan of ducks and geese can be up to 20 years, farmed birds are usually killed at only two years old. During their short lifetime, they will be plucked up to six times a year, beginning at only two months of age when they develop their first full coat. Just like sheep shearers, live rippers are paid by volume and, as a result, work as fast as they can, disregarding the pain and injuries they cause each individual bird. PETA estimates the number of live pluckings per year to be around 250,000.[20]

Photo by Ibrahim Munir

Live plucking is illegal in most countries. However, a Swedish investigative documentary that was broadcast in February 2009 confirmed that between 60 and 90 per cent of the world's down comes from live-plucked geese and ducks – a fact which was verified by an independent research study carried out by Ikea as well as an investigation by PETA.[21] Live plucking happens in the main three down-producing countries (China, Hungary and Poland) and, while international certifications such as the *Responsible Down Standard* (RDS) or the *Non Live-Plucked Products Guarantee* try to convince consumers that down and feathers do not come from live-plucked birds, they more than often do. The RDS, for example, states on its website that it 'safeguards the welfare of geese and ducks,' but has also admitted that it allows RDS certified companies to buy and sell live-plucked feathers. During the PETA investigation into down harvest in China, suppliers disclosed that buying and selling live-plucked down and misleading consumers was a common practice which makes honest investigations back to the source very difficult.

Source: VEGANDESIGN.ORG

What about 'ethically sourced' or 'humane' down? Companies selling this type of down claim that the down is 'humanely' hand collected from naturally moulting birds. Some maintain that the down is collected from the nests, while some explain ethically sourced down as the gentle removal of loose feathers by hand from a live duck or goose during moulting season. That all sounds lovely. However, it is not economically viable for any business as the moulting season is influenced by the age, breed and genetics of the bird. This means that some birds are

49

simply not moulting at the time of harvesting. Although humane down is sold at a much higher price and must be certified, the world's demand for down cannot be met by this romantic idea and the down may well still come from a supplier who lies about the feathers' origin.

Photo by Sincerely Media

Adverse Health Effects

Similar to wool, down and feathers are a perfect breeding ground for dust mites and bacteria which often lead to asthma and respiratory issues, especially in kids. Insufficient washing, storage and long-term use of feather duvets and pillows are the main conditions enabling mites to thrive. Allergies to down or feathers themselves are relatively rare; however, the number of patients suffering from adverse health effects caused by these products is increasing, with the most common symptoms resembling those of hay fever. Skin reactions such as allergic contact dermatitis, causing itchy skin, redness, dryness and raised bumps, are quite common as well. This can be led back to two types of chemicals used to treat down and feathers which pose a serious threat to the health of consumers: one is used to prepare antimicrobial-impregnated down and feather materials, the other is a group of sticky chemicals that bind dust and fibres to down clusters to increase the weight of the product.

In 2019, the story of a 43-year-old man with 'feather duvet lung' was making the rounds in the news.[22] It was explained as a lung inflammation caused by breathing in dust from down and feathers and a form of hypersensitivity pneumonitis with symptoms including night sweats, a dry cough and shortness of breath, as well as irreversible scarring of the lungs due to repeated exposure to the cause.

Down & Feather Alternatives

There are many warm, soft and light alternatives to down and feathers. While most down alternatives are made from man-made materials, the following materials are all made from natural fibres.

Kapok

Kapok is a cotton-like material that is produced by the Kapok tree. Kapok is sometimes referred to as silk cotton due to its soft and fluffy texture. This is a 100% natural fibre that is non-toxic and chemical-free.

Buckwheat Hulls

Buckwheat hulls promote and improve microcirculation, aid the prevention and treatment of cardiovascular and cerebrovascular diseases, promote sleep, ease heat, and prevent colds. The benefits and positive side effects of a buckwheat pillow may differ from person to person but are substantiated by many consumers who have found pain relief and comfort with the regular use of the pillow. A buckwheat pillow is malleable and non-shifting to allow for a contouring to your unique body shape and comfort needs. They are considered a hypoallergenic and dust-mite-resistant choice since they provide excellent airflow.

Hypoallergenic Organic Cotton (GOTS certified only)

Organic cotton is pesticide free, pigment free, bleach free and hypoallergenic. Organic cotton does not use chemicals in the manufacturing process and is therefore less likely to cause a reaction in people with chemical sensitivities.

Natural Latex (NOT synthetic latex)

The raw material for natural latex comes from a renewable resource – it is obtained from the sap of the rubber tree. Rubber trees are often cultivated through new planting and replanting programs by large scale plantations and small farmers to ensure a continuous sustainable supply of natural latex. Natural latex is both recyclable and biodegradable, and is mould, mildew and dust mite resistant. Because natural rubber has high energy production costs and is restricted to a limited supply, it is more costly than petroleum-based foam. It is important that you use natural latex and not synthetic latex though! The terminology is very confusing because synthetic latex is often referred to simply as 'latex' or even '100% natural latex'. Synthetic latex, also known as styrene-butadiene rubber, is toxic to the lungs, liver, and brain.

'Only when we have become non-violent
towards all life will we have learned to live
well ourselves.'
-Cesar Chavez

FUR

Myth 1: Fur is environmentally friendly and sustainable

Myth 2: Fur is organic

Myth 3: Fur is a natural and renewable resource

Facts

All of the above myths can be easily proven wrong. Before I get into the environmentally disastrous consequences and the health impacts of the fur industry, I will start by describing the typical life of a fur-bearing animal raised on a fur factory farm. As with all other factory animal farms, the practices in fur factory farms are designed to maximize profits, which always happens at the expense of the animals. Fur-bearing animals exploited for clothing and interior decoration, be it foxes, raccoons, minks, rabbits, chinchillas, lynxes or hamsters, lead short but very painful lives. They are packed into small cages, making it impossible for them to move more than a few steps. With cages often stacked on top of each other, the animals are urinating and defecating onto each other. The cages are exposed to the elements with no protection from heat or snow. The animals live with untreated diseases and parasites. Especially for solitary animals like minks, the overcrowding leads to anxiety, stress, frustration and other psychological hardships resulting in self-mutilation or cannibalisation of their cage mates. They pace endlessly, bite their tails and feet, and gnaw at their own skin. Water is only provided in a drop-by-drop bottle which often gets blocked or freezes in winter. Farms that breed and kill minks for fur usually breed female minks once a year, with three to four surviving kittens in each litter who are killed when they are about six months old. Minks used for breeding are generally kept for four to five years.

Killing methods at fur farms are especially gruesome as fur farmers are interested in keeping the furs intact and limiting the damage to the pelts. Some of the methods could have been taken directly from a horror movie and include the following:

- animals are stuffed into boxes and poisoned with hot, unfiltered engine exhaust from a truck which is not always lethal, resulting in some animals waking up while they are being skinned

- animals are painfully electrocuted by having clamps attached to their mouths and rods forced into their anuses or genitals

- animals are poisoned with strychnine, which suffocates them by paralysing their muscles with painful, rigid cramps

- severing heads and neck-breaking

- skinning alive

Source: VEGANDESIGN.ORG

Eighty-five per cent of traded furs come from fur factory farms which can be found all over the world – Europe, North America, China, Russia, Argentina. Millions of fur-bearing animals in the wild are also killed by steel-jaw traps every year – a method which is inhumane and banned by the European Union and a growing number of US states but widely legal in other parts of the world. While New York State was the first to ban slaughter by electrocution, there are no federal laws to protect animals on fur farms in the US and there are no penalties for abusing animals on fur farms in China, which is the world's largest fur exporter. Just like with leather, China has a strong dog and cat fur industry where cats and dogs are regularly bludgeoned and hanged and often skinned while still alive. Their fur is generally mislabelled so that it cannot be traced back to a specific kind of animal. A PETA Asia investigation of rabbit fur farms and a slaughterhouse in China found rabbits forced to live in cramped, filthy cages before finally being strung up and skinned, also often while still alive. While rabbit fur is often considered – and marketed as – a mere by-product of rabbit meat, one billion rabbits are killed every year for clothing, lures in fly fishing, or decorative items such as throws and cushions.[23]

Let us have a look at the environmental impact of fur farming. While the fur industry likes to claim that fur is environmentally friendly and sustainable, it actually causes a long list of environmental damages: waste runoff, water contamination, air pollution, biodiversity loss, local pollution, etc.[24] Fur farms all over the world are frequently reported for breaching environmental regulations. Nitrates, phosphates and other hazardous chemicals run off with rain water and pollute water supplies. Manure, left-over feed and carcasses are disposed of in wetlands, while run-off from fur farms seeps into soils and waterways causing severe damage to local ecosystems. The nutrients in manure run-off can lead to the growth of toxic algae in waterways which causes a loss of biodiversity. The algae limits the amount of oxygen for other aquatic species and creates dead zones. On top of all that, the tons of manure produced in intensive fur farms create ridiculously high greenhouse gas emissions. In Denmark alone, where more than two million minks are killed each year for their fur, more than 8,000 pounds of ammonia are released into the atmosphere every year.[25]

Another claim the fur industry likes to make is that fur is a natural and renewable resource. However, the biodiversity loss caused by fur farms and trapping is more than significant. Trapping huge numbers of fur-bearing species every year messes with the balance of nature and leads to unnatural changes in the populations of other animal species that would normally live in balance with the fur-bearing animals. Many non-target species are caught in traps, some of them classified as endangered or threatened. Historically, the fur trade has had a severe impact on biodiversity and is responsible for the depletion, and even extinction, of several furred species, including the sea mink.

In 2019, California became the first US state to ban fur sales, followed by Hawaii and Rhode Island in 2020. Forty-one mink fur factory farms in the Netherlands, three farms in Denmark and one farm in Spain have been closed down in 2020 when the animals were found to be infected with the strain that causes Covid-19, and governments ordered the slaughter of more than 2.5 million animals. Originally planning to phase out mink farms by 2024, the Dutch parliament has announced that all mink fur farms in the Netherlands will close permanently by March 2021 which has saved about 13.5 million minks from short, miserable lives and cruel deaths. Hopefully, the other countries will follow. While we are waiting for the world to follow the progress made by the Netherlands and California, let us look at how fur affects interior design and people's health.

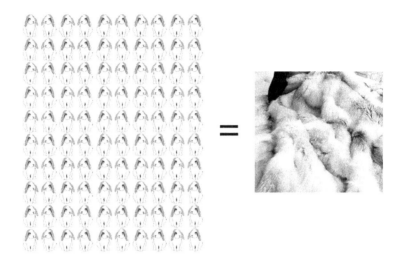

Source: VEGANDESIGN.ORG

Adverse Health Effects

Once an animal has been murdered, skin and pelt are treated with a hazardous toxic mix of chemicals and heavy metals to prevent it from rotting and decomposing. The toxins, also used for bleaching and dying pelts, pose serious health risks to the workers in fur processing plants as well as the end consumers. The World Bank actually ranks the fur industry as one of the world's five worst industries for toxic metal pollution.[26] Chemicals used in fur tanning and dressing include hydrogen peroxide, causing burns to the skin and tissue damage to the eyes; formaldehyde, linked to leukaemia; chromium, linked to cancer; ethoxylates, which can cause allergies, cancer and hormonal imbalance; and ammonia, linked to chronic irritation of the respiratory tract, asthma, lung fibrosis and

59

dermatitis. The toxins found in fur are absorbed through air or skin and can remain in the body for over twenty years, causing chronic health problems.

Fur Alternatives

There are plenty of faux furs out there, some of which look and feel amazing. They are not hard to find so if this is something you or your clients think they need, there are plenty of options. There is some controversy around faux furs (just as much as with faux leather) as many people believe that wearing it, or displaying it at home, promotes all fur and glamourises wearing the skin and coat of another animal even if it is faux. Whether this is something you support or not, I cannot personally recommend the use of faux furs with a good conscience simply for environmental reasons. Sure, they are not harming animals directly, but they are made of petroleum-based synthetic fibres such as acrylic and polyester (so essentially plastic) and not good for the environment at all – which means they are indirectly harming humans and animals alike.

'It's not hard to make decisions once you
know what your values are.'
-Roy E. Disney

SILK

Myth 1: No animals are harmed in producing silk

Myth 2: Silkworms are allowed their natural metamorphosis to be completed

Myth 3: Worms do not have the ability to experience pain

Facts

Silk is derived from the cocoons of the larvae of silkworms, who are the offspring of moths. To produce the cocoon, the moth spits out thread from tiny holes in its jaws and spins it into a little egg-bearing ball. It takes a moth about 72 hours to make one little cocoon of 500-1200 silken threads. In nature, the silkworm would go through the normal stages of metamorphosis and transform from an egg into a larva then a pupa and then an adult moth. On silk farms, however, a silkworm will not live past the pupa stage, when it will be boiled, steamed or gassed alive in its cocoon. This makes it easier to obtain a single, unbroken filament that can be woven into silk thread. Approximately 6,600 silkworms are killed to make one kilogram of silk.[27] To make this easier to imagine, it takes 360 silkworms to make one lamp shade, 12,000 silkworms to make a comforter and 48,000 silkworms to make a 14 metre curtain panel (VEGANDESIGN.ORG).

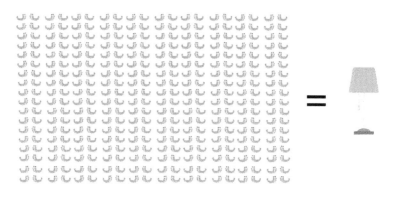

Source: VEGANDESIGN.ORG

While it is often claimed that silkworms do not have the ability to process emotional information, and therefore cannot experience pain, this has been proven wrong in multiple studies. A Swedish study published in 1979 found that worms produce two kinds of chemicals which have been identified in human brains as similar to opiates in their ability to affect sensations of pleasure and pain [28]. The production of these endorphins by a worm is believed to occur to enable the animal endure pain. A worm or moth may not get a lot of consideration as they are tiny and silent and cannot show their distress in any ways we could recognise. However, as a PETA investigation into silk points out: 'anyone who has ever seen earthworms become startled when their dark homes are uncovered must acknowledge that worms are sensitive'.[29] The investigation uncovered that even if silk farmers do not boil or gas the cocoons, they often don't provide adequate food, forcing them out of their cocoons prematurely. Producers of a so-called 'Peace Silk' claim that they let the silkworms mature naturally and only collect the cocoons once the moths have naturally emerged. However, there is no certification process in place and no authority can guarantee that normal silk is not sold as peace silk.

Apart from the animal cruelty, children as young as five years old are often forced to work in silk factories in India, the world's second largest silk producer, according to Human Rights Watch.[30] Every phase of the silk production sees children work 12 or more hours a day, six and a half or seven days a week. They burn and blister their hands while dipping them in boiling water when making silk thread; they inhale toxic fumes from machinery; they handle dead worms that cause infections; and they obtain cuts to their fingers, when winding the silk into strands, that usually go untreated and can become infected. By the time they reach adulthood, they are impoverished, illiterate and often crippled by the work.

Ranking just behind Cow Leather, silk has by far one of the worst impacts on the environment of any textile according to the Higg Index. It is even worse than cotton, using even more fresh water, causing even more water pollution and emitting even more greenhouse gases.

The biggest environmental impact after water usage and pollution is energy usage: silk farms need to be kept at a certain humidity and temperature, which requires a lot of air conditioning and humidity control as silk comes mostly from hot Asian climates. Drying the cocoons after harvesting them is usually done by using energy from coal-fired plants.

Photo by GLady

Adverse Health Effects

I have not come across any conclusive adverse health effects of using silk, but see above for the ethical and environmental facts that speak against using silk for your home.

Silk Alternatives

Banana Silk

Banana Silk is made from the inner strands of the stalks of banana plants, which are very fine and replicate the softness and sheen of silk. Its natural strength and ability to mimic traditional silk makes banana silk a very old silk alternative which has been used in Southeast Asian cultures since the 13th century. Banana fibre is eco-friendly as banana plants usually do not require the use of fertilizers or pesticides and no chemicals are needed to manufacture it.

65

Citrus Silk

Citrus Silk is made from citrus pulp, which is the wet residue that remains at the end of the industrial production of citrus juice. It reduces waste and pollution by transforming the by-products of the citrus industry into fabric. It has a silky appearance and can be printed and coloured like traditional fabrics: opaque or glossy; and pure or mixed with other yarns like cotton.

Cactus Silk

This silk alternative is made from fibres of the Agave Cacti which are quick to grow and can be replaced very quickly. Their leaves are crushed and soaked in water to separate fibres and filaments. Then the fibres are washed, dried and spun into silk threads. Cactus silk can be coloured with vegetable dyes making it free from any unnatural elements or chemicals.

Lotus Silk

Lotus silk is made of the long roots of the lotus flower. As lotus plants require very little water, flourish without the use of chemical pesticides and are generally processed completely by hand, it has little to no carbon footprint. The fabric is still quite rare and pricey, but its eco-credentials should make it surge in popularity in the coming years. If looking for it make sure it is 100% lotus as it is often blended with 'real' silk.

'You may choose to look the other way,
but you can never say again that you didn't
know.'
-William Wilberforce

TEXTILES

You may have noticed that I tried to focus on sustainable and healthy materials when talking about leather, wool, down, silk and fur alternatives. I did this for a reason. As I said at the beginning, there are a lot of grey areas and trade-offs: buying faux fur is great in that no animals have died for it; but basically all faux furs are made of one or another form of plastic and various blends of harmful chemicals.

As we all know, plastics last hundreds of years, even if they are labelled as 'biodegradable'.

I think ditching leather, wool and all other animal derived materials is the first important step for a kinder world, but if you care just as much for the environment and your personal health, we need to dive a little bit deeper into the subject of textiles.

In the production of any textile, there are basically two types of fibres: natural fibres and man-made fibres. Man-made fibres can further be divided into fibres made from petroleum and fibres made from plants. Fibres that are made from petroleum are synthetics like polyester, nylon and acrylic. They can be compared to single use plastics – they are bad for the environment and will stick around for hundreds of years polluting our planet. Fibres made from plants are called cellulosic and are textiles such as rayon or viscose. The conclusion could be that any fibre made from plants is healthier and better than fibre made from petroleum. Unfortunately, it is not that easy. Although rayon comes from cellulose, which occurs naturally in plants, it has usually undergone numerous chemical processes before it is turned into its final form.

Let us take bamboo sheets as an example: They are often sold as organic, natural and antibacterial. These qualities may well be true for the bamboo plant in its natural state. However, once the bamboo has been pulverised into fibres, which are then converted into yarn, chemicals that are harmful to the environment and to humans will usually be added. This makes the bamboo textile which the sheets are made of a man-made fabric which is neither anti-bacterial nor organic.

Photo by Mel Poole

There are many certifications out there and some of them have very confusing criteria. These are two important standards to know: The Global Organic Textile Standard (GOTS) and the Oeko-Tex Standard 100.

The Global Organic Textile Standard ensures that every step of the textile production adheres to a strict standard, from field to fashion. For example, the standard requires proper water treatment so that chemicals used in the production of textiles are not flushed into the environment. Hazardous pesticides are banned in organic cotton production, making it safer for growers. Allergenic, carcinogenic or toxic chemical residues are not allowed in GOTS certified clothes. Factories are regularly inspected and certified to strict social criteria, meaning that there is no forced labour and no child labour.

Oeko-Tex Standard 100 certified textiles are tested to be free from harmful levels of more than 100 substances known to be harmful to human health.

CONFUSED?! So how do you pick the right product, be it sheets, towels or an upholstery fabric? A good start is to pick a textile that has GOTS certification. GOTS only certifies natural fibres so you know that the fabric does not contain any man-made components. Your next best bet is a man-made textile that is made from plants and has an Oeko-Tex Standard 100 certification. On top of that, if you can, stick with products manufactured in your own country to minimize the embodied energy needed to make and transport it.

Convenience and cost are two very important factors in our everyday lives. While I would love to say that everything in my home is environmentally friendly and sustainable, it is not. All I am trying to do here is give you some tools and information and you can decide how these will work for you.

'It is just like man's vanity and impertinence to call an animal dumb because it is dumb to his dull perceptions.'
-Mark Twain

PAINT

I n Australia, the go-to wall paint for any type of project is Dulux. After finding out that their paint is not vegan, I googled 'vegan paint' in 2018. A few pages came up but all of the suppliers were located overseas, in either the UK or the US. One year later, I googled 'vegan paint' again and two new companies showed up, both local Australian businesses with explicitly vegan wall paint. Being comparable in quality and colour options, they are now the obvious choice for any of my projects. This little story just reinforces the point that I keep making: Vegan interior design products are a thing; and that thing is quickly growing!

So, what would not be vegan about regular wall paint? Standard wall paints traditionally include animal products such as casein which is the primary protein in milk, shellac which is a resin secreted from the female lac bug, or ox gall which is a wetting agent that comes from cows. Some paints use beeswax as a binder. In addition to the animal-derived ingredients, paints are often also tested on animals – which can include testing the paint on animals skin or forced ingestion.

While many paints are classified as natural or eco-friendly, that does not necessarily mean that they are vegan or cruelty-free. 'Natural' is a buzzword with no actual definition or regulation in most places and its use does not mean that there are no petrochemical ingredients. Just like with fabrics, it is always safest to check with the manufacturer first to know exactly what the paint is made of.

In terms of health, there are some other factors to look out for: titanuim dioxide is a pigment used in many paints to increase their ability to cover walls and give it opacity. However, it has carcinogenic properties and thus should not be anywhere near or around you. Water-based paint is also always the better choice as solvent- or latex-based paints contain chemicals harmful to humans. Vegan paints come with a big health benefit as they are generally less toxic with a lower concentration of volatile organic compounds (VOCs), using plant-based solvents and zero VOC colourants.

'I hold that the more helpless a creature,
the more entitled it is to protection by man
from the cruelty of man.'
-Ghandi

FLOORING

There is no vegan or non-vegan flooring per se. Just like with textiles, some are more environmentally friendly than others though, and if you are already trying to cause as little harm as possible to others and to the environment, it is worth having a look at the 'better' choices.

The most popular environmentally friendly flooring options are cork, rubber, linoleum, bamboo, reclaimed hardwood and concrete. If you hear of cork flooring and a horribly dated 80s look comes to mind, you are not alone – I was exactly the same. But the types of cork flooring available these days for residential and commercial use are surprisingly stunning, neutral looking and sophisticated. When you get to the 'Offices' chapter, you will find pictures of a beautiful little office space designed by 2LG Studio in London where they used cork for the floors and walls and it looks stunning.

Photo Credit to ReadyCork, Vita Collection

Cork

Cork is harvested from the bark of the cork oak tree. The trees do not need to be cut down to harvest the bark; it will just grow back every three years, which makes cork an ideal renewable source. Cork has anti-microbial properties that reduce allergens. It is fire retardant and low on emissions, reduces noise and acts as a natural insect repellent. It can be finished in many different stains, is easy to maintain, and can last 10 – 30 years.

Rubber

Rubber flooring is made from recycled tires and can be a versatile, beautiful and lasting option. Forget about the gym look that may just have popped up before your inner eye. Rubber is comfortable to walk on, water resistant and easy to maintain. It comes in many patterns and colour options that can look stylish in all types of residential and commercial spaces.

Linoleum

Linoleum is made from a blend of linseed oil, cork dust, tree resins, wood flour, pigments and ground limestone. It is not to be confused with vinyl flooring, which is a synthetic made of chlorinated petrochemicals that are harmful for humans and the environment. Linoleum is a long-lasting, easy to maintain flooring option that is also fire retardant and water resistant.

Bamboo

Bamboo is made from natural vegetation that grows to maturity in three to five years, which is far less than the time trees can take to grow. It is durable, sustainable and easy to maintain. Its varied grains and large spectrum of colours give it a wide area of applications.

Reclaimed Hardwood

Reclaimed wood flooring is ideal if your heart is set on real wood as it repurposes existing wood from trees that were chopped down a long time ago.

Concrete

Polished concrete is a sustainable and extremely versatile flooring option cancelling out the need for traditional flooring to be put over it. It is extremely durable, easy to clean and never needs to be replaced.

A word on carpet and rugs: wall-to-wall carpeting is difficult to clean and can quickly become a haven for dust mites, mould and mildew, which is anything but ideal for those suffering from allergies or asthma. If you want to avoid wool, you are usually stuck with alternatives made of synthetic fibres, such as polyester and nylon, which contain a myriad of toxic chemicals. There are, however, some environment- and health-friendly options which include wall-to-wall sisal, jute, seagrass and coir made from coconut husks. Similar to the wall-to-wall carpet replacement options, cotton, hemp, jute, seagrass, sisal, bamboo and linen rugs are great alternatives to wool rugs. And if these sound a bit rough and scratchy to you, let me tell you that there are some super soft ones out there these days.

Of course, if you go a step further, most dyes are usually animal-based. Just like with everything else, you have to ask the manufacturer to find out what is really in a rug apart from the natural fibres. There is no 100 per cent vegan rug manufacturer at the time of writing, but most natural fibre rug suppliers have a good choice of vegan rugs even if they are not yet labelled that way yet.

'We have decided somewhere that wool carpets are an expensive luxury item. Yes, they are expensive but I think there is something luxurious about having that choice to decide what product to have in your home. There's a luxury in that.'

Risha Walden, Walden Interiors New Jersey

'Vegan décor is the hottest trend in
Hollywood homes.'

Spaces

While materials and finishes make up the majority of any interior design project, I want to point out a few other factors that play a big part in vegan interior design, room by room or space by space.

'The secret to designing vegan decor lies in asking questions, sourcing with integrity from ethical companies and commissioning local artisans to create bespoke pieces that complement a vegan home.'

Emma Hooton, Studio Hooton London

While Sarah Barnard – award-winning interior designer, based in LA, specialising in eco-friendly design – notes that her Hollywood clientele is increasingly asking for vegan home decor due to animal welfare concerns, vegan interior design is not reserved only for the rich. There are definitely vegan options for all budgets; but I do like the position Deborah diMare takes when she says that vegan interior design products may in some cases be more costly, but they will save you just as much if not more in medical bills so it all evens out in the end.

As pointed out before, vegan interior design is as much about health and sustainability as it is about animal welfare. I discussed 'good' vs 'bad' materials; now I would like to have a closer look at some room-specific furniture and furnishings that are typically either not vegan or are terrible for your health and the planet. In this section, I also want to talk a bit about commercial interior design such as restaurants, hotels and offices. Material and furniture specifications will generally need to be more durable for commercial projects. However, the vegan interior design principles do not differ so much from residential specifications. I have therefore chosen to look more at what is happening in this space right now and what is yet to come.

'The animals of the world exist for their
own reasons. They were not made for
humans any more than blacks were made
for whites, or women for men.'
-Alice Walker

BEDROOMS

Materials and fillings, such as down and feathers, that are typical to bedroom furnishings have been discussed in previous chapters, so here I would like to summarise what to look out for when designing a healthy, sustainable and vegan bedroom.

Bed Frames and Bed Heads

A slatted wooden bed frame made from untreated natural timbers is the best option because it allows the mattress to air from underneath. If you can, avoid padded headboards and bases as they are generally filled with either wool, feathers and down, or high-density foam made of a blend of polyurethane – with a tendency to off-gas. Either way, make sure that the upholstery fabric is made from organic and natural fibres.

Mattresses

Wool and silk often hide in the upholstery layers, padding and lining of mattresses. I want to raise something very important about mattresses, though, which is not obvious to many people as marketing strategies are doing a good job misleading the public: stay away from memory foam, synthetic latex and vinyl!

Memory foam mattresses contain toxic chemicals such as formaldehyde, benzene, naphthalene and isocyanates. The latter can cause irritation of the eyes, nose, throat and skin and lead to respiratory issues such as bronchitis, tightness of the chest and asthma. The chemical flame retardants in memory foam have also been linked to developmental brain disorders, cancer and obesity.

Synthetic Latex is a man-made compound that mimics the properties of natural latex and is produced from petrochemicals. Also known as styrene-butadiene rubber, it contains the chemical styrene, which is highly toxic to the lungs, liver and brain and can cause a long list of health issues: headaches, fatigue, weakness, depression, hearing loss and increased risk of leukaemia and lymphoma. Another ingredient, butadiene, is known to harm the nervous system and cause eye and skin irritations as well as cancer. In addition to the off-gassing, petrochemicals do not deal well with moisture. The moisture given off by your body while you sleep becomes trapped in the synthetic latex, creating a breeding ground for mould, mildew and dust mites.

Mattress covers are often made with vinyl to make the mattress waterproof and hygienic, especially when it is for a cot mattress. Vinyl is nothing other than a PVC that has been softened with the help of phthalates, toxic substances which are added to increase flexibility, durability, transparency and longevity. The problem with phthalates is that they off-gas with your head right next to them – and if you think about how much time you spend on your mattress breathing in toxic gases, this poses a very big health risk. The risk is even higher for babies and young children, who spend up to 15 hours a day sleeping – more than 60 per cent of their early years. Research has linked phthalates to asthma (especially in children), ADHD, breast cancer, obesity, type II diabetes, low IQ, behavioural issues, neurodevelopmental issues, autism spectrum disorders, altered reproductive development and male fertility issues. There are many studies on the adverse health effects of phthalates, one tracing the effects of phthalate exposure on children from foetus to school-age and showing that children who were exposed to high concentrations of phthalates in the womb were 70 per cent more likely to develop asthma between the ages of 5 and 12. [31]

While long-term effects of memory foam and synthetic latex have not directly been tested, it is safe to say that you do not want to surround yourself with a myriad of hazardous chemicals that put you at risk. You may not display any effects but, at the same time, you may be waking up with headaches, develop respiratory issues or deal with long-term health effects from years of nightly exposure to these toxins – and why would you take that risk if other, healthy, alternatives are out there.

Also, generally, whenever it says 'anti-microbial' or 'anti-bacterial' on a product it means, by law, that a pesticide was added to the natural fibre and while it sounds enticing and logical to buy something with these claims, you do not want the chemicals from pesticides anywhere near you or your family.

It gets tricky when suppliers market their mattresses as 'made with 100% natural latex', 'contains natural latex' or even '100% natural latex' when what they are really selling is a blend of natural and synthetic latex with very little 'natural' content. The easiest way to get around misleading marketing claims is to stick to Global Organic Latex Standard (GOLS) certified organic latex.

Look for mattresses and casings made from natural fibres such as certified organic cotton, hemp, eucalyptus fibres or organic natural pure latex, which is inherently hypo-allergenic, dust mite resistant and super durable.

As discussed in the 'Textiles' chapter, cotton that is not certified organic has been treated with pesticides which are toxic and should not be anywhere near your skin.

Good certifications to look out for are, as usual: Global Organic Textile Standard (GOTS), Global Organic Latex Standard (GOLS) and OekoTex Standard 100; but also GreenGuard, USDA Organic and MadeSafe.

Linen

Look out for GOTS and/or OekoTex Standard 100 certifications for all fabrics you buy. As mentioned earlier in the book, bamboo sheets are not healthy or sustainable per se, especially not when the natural bamboo fibres have been treated with a myriad of chemicals to turn them into a fabric. Buying certified sheets avoids the risk that the textiles have been treated with chemicals such as formaldehyde, which is known to cause cancer and can off-gas for many years.

Pillows & Quilts

Avoid down or feathers in your bedding, not only to steer clear of animal cruelty but because they are one of the most common sources of allergies due to not being washable and a perfect breeding ground for dust mites. Natural fibres that are GOTS and/or Oeko-Tex Standard 100 certified are the best choice and include kapok, organic cotton, linen, bamboo, buckwheat hull, millet hull and hemp.

Photo by Seashell in love - Kristin

'Until one has loved an animal, a part of
one's soul remains unawakened.'
-Anatole France

LIVING ROOMS

Similar to bedrooms, typical living room furniture can easily hide animal products where you would not expect them. The following summary lists what to look out for when designing a cruelty-free living room.

Sofas

Sofas are one of the most important pieces of furniture in a space. Choosing the right one is as important as picking a good mattress. Often, while the fabric may be vegan, the seat, back or scatter cushions are still filled with down – or contain at least some down component, in the form of a wrapping underneath the fabric. Sofas are often still sold as vegan so you will need to make sure that the label does not only refer to the fabric but the entire lounge. As always, the best option is to ask the manufacturer directly and engage in a little bit of detective work. Don't be discouraged though; there are plenty of products out there, they are just not as clearly labeled yet (of course I am optimistic that this will change over the next years). The other option is, of course, to have it custom made.

'What we find hardest to replace at this stage are sofas as there is almost always at least some down component. We tend to design the lounges for our clients ourselves now and get them made rather than going shopping. It is not always easy to convince clients to pay for something they cannot see, touch and test in a showroom but we have been very successful with this method.'

Jordan Cluroe and Russell Whitehead from 2LG Studio London

Rugs

Even if you love bold and colourful patterns, there is no need to rule out natural fibres such as organic cotton, jute, hemp, silk, sisal and seagrass. These can all be woven with other materials to create a bold and graphic rug design for those looking for something more stylish and less rustic.

'The biggest challenge for me were the rugs because they are typically made of wool. The alternatives are either made of cotton dhurrie which does not have the plushness of wool or you're looking at a synthetic which is super hard on the environment as well. It is such as trade off. We ended up buying 'Perennials' which is a well-known outdoor brand in the US. The company had just released a line of rugs that were made of completely solution dyed acrylic yarns that had a cut pile similar to a standard wool cut pile and had the same feeling. They had the benefit of being pretty stain resistant and we were able to customise them.'

Tatum Kendrick, Studio HUS Los Angeles

Tony Kanal's Home in LA, Design: Tatum Kendrick Studio Hus LA

'In their capacity to feel fear, pain,
hunger, and thirst, a pig is a dog is a bear
is a boy'
-Ingrid Newkirk

KIDS ROOMS & NURSERIES

I recently interviewed Rebecca Connolly about her brand *Clever Coconuts*. Together with her husband, she developed the very successful first vegan play food set to allow for inclusive play for 'clever coconuts who eat vegan for health, the planet and the animals'. It is handmade and vegan down to the ink printed on the recycled wood. The full set comprises six different plant milks and vegan staples like tofu, vegetable burgers, tempeh, jackfruit in a can, hommus, dairy-free cheese and butter and coconut yogurt. Although the play set is not specifically an 'interior design' product such as a finish or a furniture piece, the existence and availability of a vegan play set collection demonstrates that a shift is happening even for the very small people. It shows that there is a demand for vegan products outside of supermarkets and restaurants which goes all the way to play sets for toddlers and young children who grow up in a more conscious world. Just a few days after the interview, Aldi Australia advertised wooden play food sets, including a vegan version. While I personally prefer to support the husband wife team that put so much effort into creating this inclusive play option in a 100% sustainable way, it means a lot to see that Aldi, an international supermarket giant, is getting onboard the movement as well.

Vegan play sets aside, staying clear of animal products in a nursery and toddler room only has advantages. It leaves the negative energy that inevitably comes with animal derived materials out of the child's sanctuary and helps the little one to be safer and healthier. Just like our skin, their sensitive bodies absorb all the toxins and chemicals that surround them; in fact it is proven that children are even more prone to chemical absorption than adults.[32] The wrong materials and finishes will make them vulnerable to allergies, respiratory issues, sensory issues and sleep difficulties, to name only a few.

'The average young child spends 75% of their younger years sleeping which is why it is so important to keep their sleep environment clean, safe and healthy, especially as this is such a crucial time in life for brain development. It is proven that children are more prone to chemical absorption than adults. Also, 1 in 6 children in the US has developmental or learning disabilities. Some experts believe that these issues stem to a large extent from early exposure to toxic chemicals in their environments. Studies have proven that babies are more easily exposed to high levels of chemical emissions from crib mattresses while they sleep. Body heat increases the chemical emissions from the mattresses and toxins are being released into the air they are breathing in for hours every night.'

Deborah diMare, VEGANDESIGN.ORG

A summary of the most important things to consider when designing a nursery or child's room:

Beds

A slatted wooden fame from untreated natural timbers is ideal to allow for the mattress to air from underneath. Metal bed frames should be avoided as they can attract electric fields from nearby appliances and disturb the child's sleep.[33] If possible, stay away from bunk beds because the child who sleeps on the bottom is likely to be exposed to dust mites falling from the top bunk, which is particularly bad for children with allergies. If a bunk bed cannot be avoided, the child with allergies should sleep on the top bunk.

Mattresses

The same rules that apply for mattresses as discussed in the 'Bedrooms' chapter apply to nurseries and kids' rooms. Ideal mattresses are made from natural fibres such as organic cotton, hemp, eucalyptus fibres or 100% natural pure latex (refer to the 'Bedrooms' chapter for more information about natural latex vs. synthetic latex).

Linen

Just as with all textiles on and near your family's bodies, GOTS and/or Oekotex Standard 100 certified sheets, pillow and doona covers are the ones to look out for as they contain fewer or no toxins.

Blankets & Quilts

Instead of wool, down and feathers you can buy products made of GOTS certified organic cotton, bamboo silk, soybean fibre or lyocell.

Pillows

The best alternatives to down and feathers for young humans are Kapok (also called silk cotton) and hypoallergenic organic cotton. Kapok is super soft and naturally organic, not sprayed with insecticides while growing, and not treated with chemicals at any stage. It is resistant to dust mites, moisture and mould. For other alternatives refer to 'Bedrooms'.

Rugs

Cotton, hemp, jute, seagrass, sisal, bamboo and linen rugs are great alternatives to wool rugs.

Soft Toys

Choose toys that are made of natural materials such as timber painted with plant-based dyes and natural fabrics like organic cotton, bamboo or hemp. Make sure that soft toys are filled with natural fibres rather than foam and avoid purchasing plastic and synthetic toys from cheap importers or online. A Greenpeace-IPEN study in 2011 revealed that one third of children's products made in China, producer of two thirds of the world's toys, contain heavy metals such as lead, arsenic and chromium above the acceptable limit.[34]

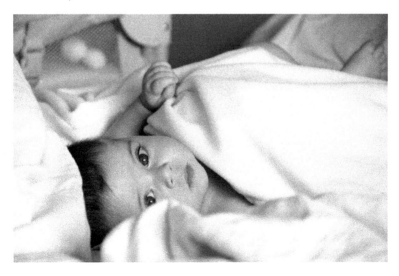

Photo by Michal Bar Haim

'Think occasionally of the suffering of
which you spare yourself the sight'
-Albert Schweizer

KITCHENS

E very project is different but, while some people design a kitchen specifically around their personal needs, there are still a lot of 'standard' kitchens and traditional ways of designing them which do not necessarily meet modern requirements.

I recently had the pleasure to talk to Boris Lauser who is a raw-plant-based chef from Germany. While he may do things on a more extensive and unique level in his kitchen than most of us, he pointed out some significant shortcomings of 'the standard kitchen' when it comes to vegan cooking and food preparation. Missing worktop space is one of the first complaints of any house owner, vegan or not. There could always be more and there is never enough! Especially for the vegan population though, there is generally not enough room for extra appliances such as blenders, high speed food processors, dehydrators and air fryers. Once you add sprouting glasses and fresh herb pots, which tend to be a bit of a staple for many, there is not really much room to actually chop and prepare anything. Dedicated sprouting stations and herb gardens higher up and away from the bench seem to be the way to go as you still want them visible so that you remember to water the plants and eat your sprouts. Smart extendable or fold-out worktops to create a temporary larger surface are very useful, as are moveable and extendable cooking islands. In addition to more space in general, the social ability of kitchens is a very important aspect. We all know people like to gather in the kitchen and I would say the majority of vegans likes to show their non-vegan friends and families how easy and delicious plant-based cooking is. If you invite your friends and family over, it is always nice to have an integrative approach, and the kitchen should allow for entertaining and gathering but also for working together. Overall, there is more need for flexibility and mobility.

Photo by Christian Mackie

Another area pointed out by Boris Lauser, which is also typically an issue for vegans and non-vegans alike, is the sink size. Sinks are generally too small but if you think of a typical plant-based diet, which generally includes a lot of fresh vegetables that need to be washed, rinsed and chopped, there is never enough space for letting vegetables drip off. While there is not always enough space for a large sink, more intelligent methods where the water gets collected would be a good approach if designing a kitchen from scratch. Whether it is a minimally tilted kitchen counter with a small ledge and water drop out or a little water collection grid so that the floor does not get flooded, it's worth getting creative and thinking outside the box.

Taking things to a more academic level, a comprehensive study exploring whether vegans have special design needs when it comes to kitchens in particular was published in 2017.[6] It is an interesting read and concludes that the vegan lifestyle requires a different approach to kitchen design due to a different style of cooking and food preparation. One important aspect the study highlights is, again, the need for more flexibility in kitchen design: 'Innovative approaches are required that are ideal for today's changing eating habits with regard to energy saving, convenience, waste reduction and biological and ecological aspects. What is of paramount importance is that one addresses the individual needs of the vegan community. As people are becoming more flexible, they also want design solutions that can be combined and adjusted to meet individual needs... Responsible consumerism is of great importance among the conscious lifestyle groups. They are less price-sensitive and willing to spend more money on products considered important for them than the general population.' [6]

In terms of specific vegan design preferences and needs the study shows that participants had an overall tendency towards natural materials such as wood or stone paired with biological resources, minimalistic design that is easy to clean and energy-saving appliances. Self-expression through design was also regarded as a good way to spread the vegan lifestyle and symbolise a healthy way of life to the outside world.

As a result of the study, Fredrik Linnér of Studiohult and Magnus Fischer of fibra developed a kitchen concept that can be applied to any kind of room. It is flexible with a wide or small version that can fold in and out and be adapted to any room shape and size. It is quite a radical design and gives us a glimpse into the future. It includes a closed water loop where fresh water comes from the tap for washing, rinsing or soaking and is then re-used for watering plants in a built-in watering shelf with a tank so that the water can be used and re-used again.

*Design & Copyright: Fredrik Linnér (studiohult.com) & Magnus Fischer
(fibra.agency)*

Obviously, tastes, preferences, needs and possibilities are very different for everyone whether they are vegan or not. Some will prefer a very traditional kitchen over a more flexible, modern design. It is worth keeping an open mind, though, and anticipating specific needs for specific groups of people, especially when their nutrition and lifestyle differs widely from the traditional ways.

'An emerging trend has developed in the segment of social media. Individuals convey the idea of a healthy lifestyle in an ever-increasing amount of blogs setting food trends for their supportive members. The adjustment in the interior market is somehow missing the opportunity. While the design of most kitchens is still like 30 years ago, it is necessary to consider what is really needed now. The expensive and lavish kitchens with two ovens and many top plates from today are often no more than superfluity. Due to the altered eating habits, design has to be adapted to the new conditions and needs of the growing target group.' [6]

Vegan Design - An Empirical Consumer Study On Kitchen Design

A kitchen related side note: Even though this may not be part of the average kitchen, fine bone china is not vegan. I am mentioning it because I have come across vegan clients who never even thought about it and were very upset when they found out. In a way you would think that it is obvious, the description contains the word 'bone', so what could well be in it? But then again, we are so used to the things surrounding us that we do not always question ingredients of household items and their ethical background. Fine Bone China contains up to 45 per cent of bone ash, usually from pigs or cows. You can, of course, pick clay or ceramic cups instead but if you really love the look and feel of fine china, look out for 'New Fine China' or 'New Bone China' (confusing I know). These alternatives replace the bone properties with 'jade' and thus make it cruelty-free.

'The most damaging phrase in the language is: "It's always been done that way"'
-Rear Admiral Grace Hopper

BATHROOMS

Even after being a pretty strict vegan for years and having designed spaces as 'strictly vegan' as I thought possible, the following revelation came to me quite late: TOWELS ARE NOT VEGAN. Well, at least most of them. When I thought about vegan design for bathrooms, only materials and appliances came to mind at first and I knew this would be pretty safe territory. I thought all I needed to educate clients in was cruelty-free hygiene and cleaning products, which are not really part of the interior design but more an extension of the overall vegan interior that people surround themselves with. I then came across a terry towelling company in Austria called Vossen who claimed to have the 'first vegan certified towel range in the world'. (Quick note: I have no affiliation with Vossen but they are the first ones making vegan towels a thing so I am using their company as an example and source.)

What could not be vegan about a towel? Here is the list that Vossen put on their website:

- Beeswax (for weaving mills and external weaving processes)
- Detergent (for wet finishing processes)
- Dyes (suspending agents for dust extraction processes)
- Polyester yarns
- Softening agents for sewing yarns
- Labels

- Booklets
- Packaging
- Glue

Since its launch in January 2019, the 'Vegan Life' range, which includes towels as well as bathrobes, has been hugely successful and Paul Mohr, CEO of Vossen, confirmed in an interview with me that after six months of research for alternative ingredients it is neither more difficult nor more expensive to produce towels in a completely vegan way. In fact, the company is now determined to make ALL of their ranges vegan by 2025.

Photo by Vossen

Another bathroom product which may come as a bit of a surprise is toilet paper... yes, that's right! Some of the most popular toilet papers are not vegan as they still contain animal ingredients like gelatin (obtained by boiling skin, tendons, ligaments and bones, usually from cows or pigs, with water) or fatty acids to bind the fibres. Many big brands cannot guarantee that the chemicals added during manufacture are not animal-derived or tested on animals. It is not too hard to find brands that confirm that their TP is vegan. It is something worth finding out, if you or your client are determined to eliminate all animal products from the home.

Other than these two bathroom staples above, there are, of course, the typical products stored and used in bathrooms such as cosmetics, hygiene articles, toothbrushes and cleaning products. As these are less 'interior design' related but rather touch daily life and routines in the home, I will not expand on them. Obviously, everything you put onto your body should be organic, cruelty-free and vegan. The same goes for everything you put onto surfaces; everything produces fumes that you breathe in so make sure there is nothing harmful hidden in the long and confusing ingredients lists. Finally, touching on the sustainability aspect: using bars of soap, shampoo, conditioner and shaving foam, rather than bottles, reduces plastic waste, as does using bamboo toothbrushes.

'Veganism is not about how hard it is for you. It's about every animal's right not to be used as a slave'
-Randy Sandberg

OFFICES

With many years of experience in commercial interior design, especially office fitouts, I know the gist. Timelines are usually sharp, the clients' ideas and expectations are unrealistic for their limited budgets, and you are competing with at least three to five other companies to even get the job. Fancy concepts and innovative mood boards are created, you win the job and a stressful period starts. I love these jobs, don't get me wrong, but looking back at the younger me working away at my desk at a Sydney interior design studio, the last thing I would have needed – on top of all of the normal requirements for an office design project – would have been the requirement for furniture and finishes to be vegan. These jobs are fast paced and money driven; people usually go for an innovative, pleasing look with a few quirky extras and some fun colours thrown in where it fits.

Photo by Nastuh Abootalebi

Knowing what I know now, though, I realise that it is just another specification. Each project has its own unique specifications, be it the allergies of a residential client or specific requirements to represent the business culture in an office space. There is really no big difference between searching for a commercial grade vegan fabric and an upholstery fabric with properties such as a super high rub count or a salt water resistance. And yes, you may need to get the breakout room lounges made, rather than buying them off the shelf, to make sure that they do not contain any wool or feathers; but chances are that the lounges would have been a specialist joinery job anyway due to specific space or company requirements. Knowing that vegan furniture and finishes are actually more available and growing exponentially, makes designing a vegan office so much easier than you may think.

Fact is that office culture is changing everywhere and, with veganism growing in popularity in all parts of the world, there is also increasing pressure for employers to make the workplace more inclusive.[35] In light of changes to UK anti-discrimination law in January 2020 which confirmed that ethical veganism is a belief that is protected within the scope of the 2010 Equality Act and now protects 'ethical veganism', The Vegan Society published a guide for employers on how to create a more inclusive work environment for vegan employees. While this does not include vegan interior design or office fitouts as such, it shows an increased awareness around veganism at the workplace.

In the US, the group Vegan Leaders in Corporate Management contributes significantly in moving this culture shift forward on a corporate level and provides a platform that supports influential vegans working in large corporations, encouraging them to advance vegan initiatives at work. Millennials are the strongest drivers and the biggest group of adopters of vegan living in the workplace environment, but the younger generations are not the only driving force. Corporations have more and more of an interest in demonstrating their commitment to diversity, inclusion, sustainability and employee wellbeing to make their company an attractive place to work. The vegan initiatives undertaken are still mainly nutrition based but they do extend to the worker's environments as well.

- Sending out a dietary requirements sheet to staff for catered events.
- Keeping kitchen utensils clean, providing color-coded equipment and separate food preparation areas.
- Offering dedicated food storage areas for vegan, such as shelves in the fridge.
- Ensuring access to vegan-friendly clothing, such as synthetic safety boots or a non-leather phone case.
- Exempting vegans from attending corporate events such as horse racing, or others which revolve around animal products, such as a "hog roast" BBQ.
- Considering exempting vegans from participating in the buying (or signing off on the purchase) of non-vegan products.
- Supporting vegan employees to discuss their pension investment options with a relevant member of staff.
- Creating a positive and respectful atmosphere towards vegan employees, for example by being mindful of "jokes" which could be deemed offensive.
- Training staff on anti-discrimination law, highlighting to them that veganism is an example of a non-religious belief protected under this legislation.
- Reassuring vegan employees that they should not feel anxious about raising complaints and that they will be taken seriously if they do so.
- Taking prompt action on unfair treatment of, or complaints from, vegans.
- Seeing how vegans can contribute to workplace policies and practices.

Vegan Society's 'Supporting veganism in the workplace: A guide for employers' [36]

In terms of interior design products – finishes, materials, furniture and furnishings – the rules and advice are not so different from the advice given in the previous chapters. There are a few things to look out for such as the filling and padding of task and executive chairs: just like in lounges, even if the fabric is a faux-leather or natural fibre, the filling could still have wool or down components so, as always, it is worth contacting the manufacturer directly to find out what a chair is made of.

Most of the major upholstery suppliers around the globe have a good choice of commercial-grade fabrics that do not contain animal products and are just as luxurious and durable as their animal-abusing counterparts.

Photos by Megan Taylor, Design by 2LG Studio London

'If you really care about animals, then stop trying to figure out how to exploit them 'compassionately'. Just stop exploiting them.'
-Gary Francione

HOTELS

W hen it comes to vegan accommodation, many hotels promote themselves as partly or even 100% vegan but, if you look a little bit deeper, what they usually mean is vegan food. There is a famous hotel in Sydney which is advertised as 100% vegan in plenty of vegan forums and websites but when I went to interview the manager about how they implemented vegan interior design in all of their rooms and spaces, I found out that it is actually the hotel restaurant that is 100% vegan, not the hotel itself.

While they are still few and far between, fully vegan hotels – or at least fully vegan hotel suites– are starting to pop up everywhere. The vegan suite of London's Bankside Hilton Hotel is probably one of the most celebrated vegan interior designs of the last years. When I was talking to Bompas & Parr, the design studio who created the suite, they said that 'the Vegan Suite was developed in response to the zeitgeist with ever more people considering veganism as an important part of their life'. Central to the design of the suite is Piñatex pineapple leather. This reinforces the overall design motif of the pineapple, which is due to the proximity of the hotel to the first site in the UK where pineapples were grown and the fruit's history as a symbol of welcome. Guests can enjoy a vegan stay from the moment they check in with upholstered Piñatex seating in the reception and a key card also made from the material. The headboard is made from pineapple leaves and embroidered by local artist Emily Potter; the flooring is made of bamboo; cotton carpets replace wool; foot stools and scatter cushions are covered with Piñatex; and pillows are stuffed with a choice of organic buckwheat, millet hulls, kapok or bamboo fibres instead of feathers. All toiletries, snacks, drinks and cleaning products used by the hotel's staff are free of animal products, extending even to the stationery which is entirely vegan-friendly with no animal traces in the paper or ink.

Photo: Hilton Bankside

Bompas & Parr added: 'Guest experience was paramount to our considerations throughout. While there has been a drive to increasingly design for instagram and visual aesthetic, we wanted to create a suite with deeper resonance, ongoing meaning and purpose for the future. Creating a suite with a strong ethos has been crucial. The results have been spectacular, both in terms of press and occupancy'.

Photo: Hilton Bankside

Another great example which was built in a 'vegan way' from scratch is Koukoumi Hotel in Mykonos. The inspiration for this 100% vegan hotel was simple and innocent: the owners wanted to preserve Mykonos' natural beauty and architecture, which nowadays becomes endangered due to extensive development, while caring for the environment and all living beings at the same time. Georgia Kontiza, General Manager and Owner of Koukoumi Hotel, says:

Since we were also the constructors of the building, we knew we could make it happen starting from scratch, taking care of even the slightest detail. Koukoumi Hotel is the proof that you can enjoy life in style, in beautiful surroundings without harming neither animals nor nature. The Greek market is rather unaware of vegan materials and fabrics. It was not always easy to find natural material completely void of animal by-products that would be organic and/or environmentally friendly at the same time. For example, we had to arrange a special tailor-made order from Cocomat to create a mattress containing only coconut fibre, natural latex, seaweed and cotton.

Photo: Koukoumi Hotel Mykonos

Veganism is a relatively new trend in Greece but it is constantly growing. Koukoumi hotel was created to cater for the needs of people who consider life and health as primordial values and believe in compassion and respect. 'Many people thought it would be too risky, but for me and my team it was a dream come true' says Manolis Xenakis, Hotel Manager at Koukoumi.

Both Georgia and Manolis described the design and building process of the hotel as a very creative and rewarding process as they found collaborators equally enthusiastic to support the project, stating that it was something the Greek market was lacking. Their advice is to never compromise, to believe in your ideal and stick to it until the very end as people will appreciate your efforts and reward you with respect. 'It is very difficult to set a new moral standard in a hostile environment but we feel like pioneers: we are carving the road that others may follow'.

Photo: Koukoumi Hotel Mykonos

'Could you look an animal in the
eyes and say to it, 'My appetite is more
important than your suffering'?
-Moby

RESTAURANTS

I t would only make sense for the many vegan restaurants that are popping up like mushrooms all over the world to have a fully vegan interior as well. While vegan nutrition is skyrocketing, the concept of making the whole space fully vegan is still foreign to some. It is simply logical to do so, though, since vegan materials and products are not only animal friendly but also much healthier as we have seen in the previous chapters. And there is absolutely no reason why a vegan restaurant would not be able to have fully vegan interiors either – it is so easy. Finding highly durable upholstery alternatives to leather and wool and using vegan paint is pretty straightforward. Pairing these with elements such as reclaimed tiles, recyclable sheet flooring and FSC certified timber furniture and joinery – like Brighton interior designer Chloe Bullock did for the restaurant Nostos in Hove – creates a cruelty-free but also sustainable and healthy environment for diners.

Little Pine Restaurant owned by Moby, Design Tatum Kendrick Studio Hus

'It really wasn't that hard to find alternatives for everything you normally specify. There is just so much on the market right now. In general, designing a fully vegan project was not so different from any other project, each project has its own limitations. I think having done two vegan projects now, it was really about finding alternatives that are really durable and that work. It's trying to find really good quality materials that have the same strength. It may be slightly more research than normal but that's all.'

Tatum Kendrick, Studio HUS Los Angeles about designing 'Little Pine' owned by Moby

Nostos Hove Restaurant, Photos: Jim Stephenson @clickclickjim, Design: Chloe Bullock

'Never doubt that a small group of thoughtful, committed citizens can change the world; indeed, it's the only thing that ever has'
-Margaret Mead

Outlook

Now if this book has helped you to work out what you want to get rid of and what you want to replace it with, be it just a mattress or a whole living room fit out, awesome! If you are motivated to create a healthy and cruelty-free sanctuary but don't know where to start, join our exclusive Facebook group 'The Vegan Interior Design Tribe' or reach out through our website www.veganinteriordesign.com.

'Many people like to make changes in distinct stages. They stay at one stage for a while, get comfortable there, and then marshal their resources for moving on to the next. Some vegans worry that nobody will ever make it all the way with this approach, but psychologists who study human behavior have noted that becoming grounded in a small change is the surest indicator that someone will go on to the next phase, to a deeper commitment. This isn't a competition, though. The idea is to do this, either all at once or in stages, in a way that's comfortable and fun, improves your health, makes sense in your actual life, and lasts forever. If you need to take forty days (or forty weeks or longer) to fully make the switch, take it...' [37]

Victoria Moran in 'Main Street Vegan'

We operate internationally and can also recommend vegan interior designers in most parts of the world. You may think hiring a professional interior designer is expensive. However, it really is not a luxury but will actually save you money. Working with a good and experienced designer helps you to avoid big and costly mistakes. Designers have a large network of suppliers and are always in touch with them about their latest ranges and products. This will save you a lot of time, especially when it comes to vegan interior design. You do not need to spend hours and days contacting manufacturers and asking them about the materials and manufacturing processes of their products as the designer will do that for you.

To send you off, I want to say it one last time: it may not be possible to live a 100% vegan life. Simple everyday things such as toilet paper and towels are generally not vegan. Many plastic shopping bags contain slip agents made of animal fat to reduce the friction in the material. Many car and bike tires are created using stearic acid which is often derived from animal grade products. Even toothpaste contains glycerin which can be found in animal fats. But to try and do your best is better than not trying at all. It's about taking steps to be better and acting more consciously, kindly and compassionately one step at a time.

Whether it is changes in your own home or business or for a clients', liaising with decision makers, contacting retailers, asking manufacturers about ingredients and procedures and challenging designers – we can all do our little bit!

Bibliography

1.   Fox, K. (2017). *Here's Why You Should Turn Your Business Vegan In 2018.* Forbes Magazine. https://www.forbes.com/sites/katrinafox/2017/12/27/heres-why-you-should-turn-your-business-vegan-in-2018/#3089362b2144

2.   Beachy, J. (2014). *The Rise of Veganism: Start a Revolution!* www.toprntobsn.com/veganism 11/2016.

3.   *The Vegan Society, Statistics*, https://www.vegansociety.com/news/media/statistics#:~:text=The%20number%20of%20vegans%20in,150%2C000%20(0.25%25)%20in%202014.

4.   Meyer, M. (2019). *How Many Vegans Are In The World?* Published online at WTVOX, https://wtvox.com/sustainable-living/2019-the-world-of-vegan-but-how-many-vegans-are-in-the-world/

5.   VEGANDESIGN.ORG (2019). *Vegan Design 101 Course*

6.   Dietrich, M., Fischer, M., Walcher, D. (2017). *VEGAN DESIGN - Do conscious nutrition groups, such as flexitarians, vegetarians and vegans, have special design needs? An empirical consumer study on kitchen design.*

7.   Hildmann, A. (2012). *Vegan for Fit.* Becker Joest Volk, 4TH Edition

8.   Harari, Y.N. (2015). Industrial farming is one of the worst crimes in history. *The Guardian.* https://www.theguardian.com/books/2015/sep/25/industrial-farming-one-worst-crimes-history-ethical-question

9.   Food and Agriculture Organizations of the United Nations (2006). *Livestock's Long Shadow: environmental issues and options*

10. PETA Australia: *Sheep Farming and the Wool Industry's Damaging Environmental Impact*

11. PETA: *Leather: Animals Abused And Killed for Their Skins*

12. Popham, P. (2000). How India's sacred cows are beaten, abused and poisoned to make leather for high street shops. *The Independent*

13. *Earthlings* (2005), http://www.nationearth.com/

14. Maurice, J. (2001). *Tannery pollution threatens health of half-million Bangladesh residents.* published in Bulletin of the World Health Organisation 79(1)

15. World Health Organization, International Programme on Chemical Safety, Environmental Health Criteria 242 (2014). *Dermal Exposure.*

16. PETA Australia. *Exposed: Australia Wool Industry Continues to Abuse Sheep* https://www.peta.org.au/action/exposed-australian-wool-industry-continues-abuse-sheep/

17. PETA UK. *Crying Alpacas Thrown and Cut for Jumpers and Scarves.* https://www.peta.org.uk/features/alpaca-wool/

18. PETA Australia. *Cashmere Industry Exposed: Terrified Goats Scream in Pain.* https://www.peta.org.au/action/cashmere-industry-exposed-terrified-goats-scream-in-pain/

19. Fransen, M., Overgaard, L., Johansen, J., Thyssen, J. (2017). *Contact allergy to lanolin: temporal changes in prevalence and association with atopic dermatitis.* https://onlinelibrary.wiley.com/doi/full/10.1111/cod.12872

20. PETA. *Down Production: Birds Abused for Their Feathers*

21. Human Decisions (2018). *The Terrible Truth About Down* https://animalpeopleforum.org/2019/10/08/the-terrible-truth-about-down/

22. Clarke N. *Down Pillow Allergy Symptoms.* Livestrong.com. https://www.livestrong.com/article/258868-down-pillow-allergy-symptoms/

23. PETA Asia. *Rabbits Hit, Hung Up, and Skinned Alive in the Chinese Fur Trade.* https://investigations.peta.org/china-rabbit-fur/

24. Fur Free Alliance. *The Environmental Costs & Health Risks of Fur.* https://www.furfreealliance.com/environment-and-health/

25. Glydenkæne, S., Mikkelsen, M. (2007). *Projection of the Ammonia Emission From Denmark From 2005 Until 2025.* Research Notes From NERI, No.239 2007, 23-9.

26. Tansy Hoskins. (2013). Is The Fur Trade Sustainable? *The Guardian* 29 Oct. 2013.

27. PETA UK. *The Silk Industry.* https://www.peta.org.uk/issues/animals-not-wear/silk/#:~:text=Even%20silk%20producers%20who%20don,out%20of%20their%20cocoons%20prematurely.

28. Alumets. J. et al. (1979). Neural localisation of immunoreactive enkephalin and β-endorphin in the earthworm. Published in British Journal *Nature*

29. PETA Asia. *The Truth About Silk.* https://www.petaasia.com/issues/clothing/silk/#:~:text=Although%20worms%20can't%20show,a%20physical%20response%20to%20pain.

30. Human Rights Watch (2003). *Small Change: Bonded Child Labor in India's Silk Industry* https://www.hrw.org/report/2003/01/22/small-change/bonded-child-labor-indias-silk-industry

31. Whyatt, R.M. et. al (2014). *Asthma in Inner-City Children at 5–11 Years of Age and Prenatal Exposure to Phthalates: The Columbia Center for Children's Environmental Health Cohort* https://ehp.niehs.nih.gov/doi/10.1289/ehp.1307670

32. Landrigan, P.J., Goldmann, L.R. (2011). *Children's Vulnerability To Toxic Chemicals: A Challenge And Opportunity To Strengthen Health And Environmental Policy.*

33. Bjilsma, N. (2012). *Healthy Home, Healthy Family*

34. Greenpeace-Ipen (2011). *Children's products in China- Toxic heavy metals found in children's products on the Chinese market.* https://ipen.org/site/children%E2%80%99s-products-china

35. McKeever, V. (2020). *Vegans want to change the workplace ... and it all starts in the kitchen.* https://www.cnbc.com/2020/02/25/vegan-friendly-offices-tips-on-how-to-make-workplaces-more-inclusive.html

36. The Vegan Society (2020). *Supporting veganism in the workplace: A guide for employers*

37. Moran, V. (2012). Main Street Vegan: Everything You Need to Know to Eat Healthfully and Live Compassionately in the Real World.

About the Author

Aline Dürr is an award-winning interior architect, thought leader, author and voice for the voiceless. She is the founder and director of Vegan Interior Design. She has a corporate background and moved from Berlin to Sydney 10 years ago to change her career to where her passion lies. Well versed and highly experienced in building biology and healthy home design, Aline has been an interior design professional in the commercial sector for many years. She is also active in animal rescue, a dedicated foster parent to countless ex-battery hens and mother of a young girl and many rescue animals.

DO YOU WANT TO LEARN MORE?

Check out our online courses

MINI COURSES:

- VEGAN MATERIALS & FINISHES 101
- DESIGN A VEGAN HOME
- COMMERCIAL INTERIOR DESIGN
- HOW TO FIND & SIGN A VEGAN CLIENT

6 WEEK COURSE:

THE VEGAN INTERIOR DESIGN METHOD

Head to **www.veganinteriordesign.com**
for more course details and registration.

CPSIA information can be obtained
at www.ICGtesting.com
Printed in the USA
BVHW021025140721
R12407400002B/R124074PG611472BVX00021B/1